Affiliate Marketing

The Ultimate Guide to Start Making Money Online. Discover Profitable Strategies, Choose the Right Network, Learn How to Attract Traffic and Maximize your Profits.

Philip Hayes

The information herein is offered for informational purposes solely and is universal as such. The presentation of the information is without a contract or any type of guarantee assurance.

The trademarks that are used are without any consent, and the publication of the trademark is without permission or backing by the trademark owner. All trademarks and brands within this book are for clarifying purposes only and are owned by the owners themselves, not affiliated with this document.

Table of Contents

Introduction

Smart entrepreneurs operating a successful business realize that they can still do more to expand that company. One way to move it to the next step is to find an alternative income source. That doesn't mean creating a second company but searching for ways to complement and expand your company by giving your clients and followers more benefits.

It's time to start taking benefit of this attractive income stream if you're not interested in affiliate marketing.

Affiliate marketing is a famous strategy to drive sales & generate valuable online income. The modern push toward less conventional marketing techniques has paid off, which is highly beneficial for both labels and affiliate marketers. Actually:

- The influence of affiliate marketing is leveraged by 81 percent of brands and 84 percent of publishers, a figure that will continue to grow as affiliate marketing investment rises in the United States per year.

- In 2018, the cost of content marketing was estimated to be 62% of conventional marketing schemes, while creating three times the leads of traditional methods at the same period. In reality, the influence of affiliate marketing can be attributed to 16 percent of all online orders.

- In March of 2017, the affiliate structure of Amazon modified, giving rates 1 to 10% of product revenue for creators, allowing affiliates the ability to significantly raise their passive earnings depending on the vertical on which they sell.

- In June and July 2017, Jason Stone's affiliate marketing, known professionally as Millionaire Coach, was liable for approximately $7 million in retailer sales.

You've already aware about many forms of marketing: pay-per-click, email marketing, inbound marketing, marketing on social media, and so on. But now you might be wondering what affiliate marketing is?

Chapter: 1 Affiliate Marketing

"It is the mechanism through which an affiliate earns a commission by promoting the products of other people's, through different channels."

Affiliate marketing is a rising industry: for 2017, affiliate marketing investment is projected at 5.4 billion dollars in the US alone, and it's rising each year. There're many methods to gain a profit by placing affiliate links to your website, which is the most popular one.

You gain a commission when anyone buys that product via that link.

There are many necessary and crucial steps you must take before and these are not passive. The assumption is that if you are prepared to do this task and are willing to put in effort and time, so you are already well on the path for the growth of affiliate marking.

Now you have definitely decided that you can take two roles in this system: merchant or affiliate.

What task you choose depends on your objective; you can become a merchant if you have a product, and earn money by using affiliates to promote the goods. On the other side, if you want to earn money from selling goods through advertisement. you can become an affiliate.

Although most people start taking the affiliate path and it is obviously the easier path to take, it is not easy or quick to build enough traffic to make a significant income from just affiliate sales.

1.1 Fundamentals of affiliate marketing

Now, discuss the fundamentals of affiliate marketing. This can be much more advanced, but we will start a general layout for bringing in payouts. There are five steps, which are as follows

- Firstly, you identify a product that you want to promote.

- Secondly, you search your product name affiliate program (If it is on Amazon, you may even promote it)

- For their affiliate program, sign up

- You get a special link that helps the merchant to check the people who have clicked on your link.

- Now, you earn some commission on the sales when someone purchases the product via that link.

1.2 Is it useful for a business?

Affiliate marketing is a dynamic solution as well as a cost-effective way to advertise and develop new leads for the business. Therefore, the amount of money wasted on advertisement is limited because most businesses required initial investment and, with the passage of time, more financing to operate the business.

To get information about your business, you don't have to invest a lot of money. This type of marketing makes highly suitable and helpful for up-and-coming businesses that do not have a huge budget. Increase development and brand recognition. An affiliate network will help improve traffic and expand the audience online.

1.3 Main Players in Affiliate Marketing?

There are 3-4 main players who must be involved.

1. Affiliate (Publisher)

2. Merchant (advertiser, retailer, brand)

3. Consumer

   And, according to some concepts, the fourth one is:

4. Network

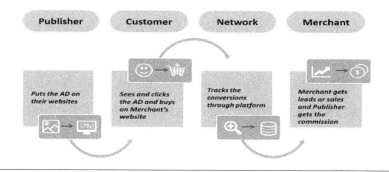

Four core players of affiliate marketing

1. Affiliate

It is also known as the publisher; the affiliate may be either a person or an entity that promotes the distributor's goods and services to prospective customers in an attractive manner. The affiliate promotes the goods to consumers that it is useful and favorable to them and persuades them to buy the goods. If the consumer buys these goods, the affiliate earns a profit.

Affiliates also help by posting items such as reading articles, creating images, videos, and other marketing campaigns.

2. Merchant (advertiser, retailer, brand)

The merchant is a vendor, product maker, or manufacturer with a product to market, whether it is a single entrepreneur or a huge corporation. The item may be tangible goods such as buildings, vehicles, household items etc. or intangible products such as insurance policy, goodwill, trademark etc.

3. Consumer

Consumers are those who purchase the merchant's product through an affiliate. Affiliate share merchant's product with the consumer on websites, blog and social media. When the consumer will complete the buying process and obtain the goods, the merchant & affiliate share the profit.

4. Network

The network is the agent between the affiliate and the merchant. It generally handles the goods delivery and payment.

Affiliates sometimes also have to utilize partner networks to be able to sell goods. There are many affiliate networks for earning passive income, but Amazon Associates is among the most famous affiliate network.

1.4 How Cookies fit in?

A cookie is a tiny piece of code inserted on the customer's computer by clicking the link from the affiliate website to your website's shopping cart. The affiliate's cookie is acknowledged as the transaction source until the transaction is done and is compensated with the commission.

1.5 What can be promoted?

AS WE DISCUSS ABOVE, AFFILIATE MARKETING IS THE MECHANISM OF GENERATING A COMMISSION BY SELLING OTHER PERSONS' GOODS (OR COMPANIES). FIRST, YOU FIND A PRODUCT WHICH YOU WANT TO SELL AND HOW YOU PROMOTE IT. You still ask yourself the following questions while trying to decide what to promote:

• Can I use this item?

• Would it help the huge percentage of my readers to use this product?

• Is it easy to purchase?

• Is there an affiliate commission rate that is good?

If the response to all these questions is yes, it is definitely a good choice and worth promoting. Create a list of the items you use to feel your blog audience will also profit from utilizing. Try to think about as many of them as possible.

And also, note that they may also contain complementary items. For example, if you write about travel, you should have many complimentary things, such as water bottles, baggage, clothes, headphones etc.

1.6 How to find opportunities?

Seeking affiliates is a mixture of actually asking individuals and letting the organization know of interested people. Moreover, by delivering outstanding goods, top-notch customer support, and a generous incentive, you will inspire customers to be affiliates.

1. Directly Contact

Find rivals and those that sell goods to your customers but do not have and specifically approach the same goods or services that you do. Act first by group efforts, gatherings, and more to make relationships with these individuals in online communities, and you will be certain to get a portion of them to sign up with your affiliate program and advertise your goods and services.

2. Internet Ads

Another approach to draw affiliates is to advertise the program and its advantages.

To monetize the program, you may use Twitter, Facebook or Ad words. This works quite well, if you have a strong sales funnel, have outstanding commissions, and a wide variety of goods for your niche

3. Print Publications

You can advertise in printed media, such as home magazines and other publications dedicated to those who are attentive in this form of income potential.

4. Shakers and Movers

You've seen them on Email, Facebook groups, and likely on various tutorials, etc., Movers & Shakers. Those major earners shake up the material. Try to build a friendship with them, then make promoting the goods super easy for them. Offering to set up everything for them so that all they have to do is raise the money when they make sales.

5. Blogging

Use the blog to chat to prospective affiliates most of the time. Your blog offers answers to their questions for your viewer. But, once you have an affiliate network, you can also address how you want to support as many more people as possible, and your readers will help by being an affiliate.

6. Consumers

Your strongest affiliates will come from individuals who have bought from you. Surely, run an email sequence for your clients by promoting your family and friends' items to enable them to earn income. This is an ideal way to wind up as an affiliate for a real follower.

7. Co-workers

You are usually part of a community of like-minded people online or offline, even though you are work from home. Make sure that you let those individuals know you have an affiliate program such that if they choose to, they may decide to participate. Special incentive amounts may also be granted to individuals you meet.

Chapter: 2 History of Affiliate Marketing?

To become a successful affiliate marketer, need to know the history of affiliate marketing, how it began to be, how it developed and improved over time. The right ones to forecast the future are those who understand the past history.

Today, most people think about affiliate marketing as an online phenomenon, but the truth is that the internet was preceded by affiliate marketing. Though, much affiliate marketing is conducted online as of today and for a very good cause.

2.1 Start before the Internet:

Affiliate marketing has been defined as something which happens online. You open a link that leads you to an online website or product, and then a small amount is paid to the link owner for that click. It may also refer to offering a customer a benefit to be referred to a new customer by a mechanic. By getting a discount on their purchase, the individual who refers is paid. It's the same theory, just in the actual world. This type of affiliate marketing is used but is not detected as often as online links/web connections. In an attempt to understand more about where your consumers came from, you might ask your customer where they learned about you, but in the end, you don't have all the details as you will with an online tracking link. The internet has made ads of this sort more profitable and simpler for your company to grow. While the past of affiliate marketing actually starts before the internet, it is the internet that has rendered this marketing technique readily accessible to the masses as a business model.

2.2 Introduction of WEB

It was an entirely different idea when the internet came along. Who ever knew that you might be linked to the whole world with only a couple of clicks? This was made possible by the internet. To make a sale, you didn't have to depend on your geographical region anymore. You can sell anything to someone in any part of the world. This made the whole method a lot more interesting and exciting and pushed things to a whole new level. Modern marketing strategies had to be created to integrate all the various areas of the world

2.3 Background of Affiliate Marketing

The affiliate marketing patent was given to William J. Tobin in 1989, as we know it today. Tobin founded PC Flowers Inc. in 1989 and began the first affiliate program designed to market his Prodigy network products. PC Flowers Inc. paid a commission to Prodigy on every transaction.

Prodigy is an internet service that offers a large range of services for paying users. This contains news, inventories and weather details, e-shopping, news, stocks and many more. In essence,

Prodigy initiated the idea of a detailed online information platform.

Among the first e-commerce providers on Prodigy was PC Flowers Inc. More significantly, it was the first to be a major financial success. Over the years, the innovative idea of Tobin created millions of dollars for Prodigy in earnings. In 1996, Tobin sought a patent on monitoring and affiliate marketing. On October 31, 2000, a patent was granted.

Tobin launched PC Flowers & Gifts, an online store for flowers and gift products, in 1994. The corporation offered affiliate services for many broad websites via Tobin's patents. By 1998, there were over 2700 affiliate marketing partners at PC Flowers & Gifts.

2.4 First Affiliate Networks

Clickbank & Commission Junction, the first affiliate network, was established in the year 1998. This encouraged small businesses unrelated to Amazon to participate the affiliate marketing game. Currently, to this day, Clickbank & Commission Junction are very successful. On a global level, they are also among the leading providers of affiliate marketing services.

Networks of affiliates act as an intermediary between affiliates and merchants. To access the network, companies seeking to expand their customer base may pay a charge. The network reimburses the affiliates for their produced sales leads.

Affiliates may, as a policy, free access to the networks. Usually, merchants are required to pay a certain fee. Affiliate networks perform well for those organizations that lack funding for large-scale outreach campaigns.

2.5 Amazon

As a program that was accessible to the general public, Amazon was the first entity to use affiliate marketing. Their scheme, known as the Associates Program, made it easier for individuals to sign up to provide links on their website. In 1996, it was released. The user was paid a little sum of money to recommend new clients due to exchanging the links to Amazon's products. Amazon was the first massive company in the history of affiliate marketing to utilize affiliate marketing as one of their marketing channels broadly. For other affiliate companies, this is the framework to base their programs, and the rise in affiliate marketing continues today.

2.6 Cookies

In 1994, the innovation of cookies by a programmer named Lou Montulli. This granted the right to track success in affiliate marketing more specifically. It's now one of the most often used ways of monitoring.

Cookies are tiny data files that are kept on people's computers when viewing a specific site. The aim is to find users and store login details for the web. They may monitor what users are doing and collect knowledge regarding their interests and activities on the site. This, in fact, makes them valuable for producing targeted ads that fit individual user profiles.

Chapter: 3 Affiliate network

The Affiliate Network module can help you create income with the assistance of an outer deal power our associates can bring. Utilize the advertising force affiliates to sell more and increment your income and shopper base. Vendors in 2 Checkout organizations make up to 25% of their income through affiliates.

The Affiliate Network can assist you:

- Boost deals. As per insights from the 2 Checkout framework, a shipper selling standard programming can build deals by 10% to 15% on normal when utilizing the Affiliate Network of 2 Checkout.

- Associate yourself with solid voices in the business, for example, MajorGeeks, Softonic, Cnet, and many more.

- Get the overall item and brand knowledge. Our associates communicate in each language on the planet and can prescribe your items to their nearby or overall crowds.

- Have your items sold by different organizations working with 2 Checkout. See strategically pitching for additional subtleties.

3.1 Getting started with the Affiliate Network

Network Settings

ENABLE THE AFFILIATE NETWORK MODULE

1.   Visit the Affiliate Network ➔ then Settings.

2.   Decide how you will support your affiliates.

- Affirm manually every affiliate (you are required to occasionally audit Pending Relationships segment and examine affiliate organization demands). By picking a Manual endorsement strategy, you can channel the affiliates in the program and spotlight on creating associations with ones that coordinate your necessities without much of a stretch.

- Let 2 Checkout affirm them consequently following an audit cycle.

Commission

Determine the commission you will offer for each fruitful deal (pay-per-deal model). The basic commission is 25%. You can offer up to 75% commission to associate. As per your strategy, you can modify the offered commission. In the not so far future, the whole settings described here will be altered at some stage. Ask 2Checkout directly on the possibility that you choose to give membership commissions greater than 75%.

3.2 Affiliates network settings

In this segment, it has three alternative menus.

1. General Settings of Affiliates Network.

The underlying General Settings of Affiliates Network designed to enact the module. The default treat life is set to awake for 120 days and addresses the timespan, during which you will grant your associates a bonus for deals they allude to. The commencement for the subsidiary treat life begins when customers click on partner joins. You can change treat life from 30 to 180 days. For example, if the treat life is set at 120 days and the alluded deal occurs following 110 days, the associate gets the commission. On the off chance that the deal occurs following 130 days, the subsidiary doesn't get any commission for that specific reference. Tip: From our information, most of the buys occur inside the initial 24 hours, however for the members' solace, you can set the treat life to its most extreme: 180 days.

2. Affiliates Joining Settings.

Characterize the commission records your subsidiaries are naturally allowed through Link Source. For instance, if you plan a promoting effort offering a particular commitment to new members, you will want to relegate all new partners to a characterized commission list consequently. All associates recruits from the connection indicated in the Link Source field will be relegated to the commission show you recently made for this mission. Associates join connections, and pages can be made from the Build your organization menu.

3. Create/alter a list of commissions.

When initiating the Checkout affiliate module, you will create the commission list: "Default List." You can either alter or make one or many new commission records dependent on the items you sell through partners. A similar item can be allocated to more than one rundown. The default commission for a rundown is 25%, yet you can transform it as indicated by your arrangement.

You have the likelihood to characterize various commissions for each buy type:

- New buys

- Trials (first buy with a preliminary client procurement model; Trial can be free or paid and time for testing can be altered, least period of 7 days, 30 days default period)

- Trial transformations (the main change after the modified time for testing lapses)

- Renewals (the principal charging cycle after the preliminary change in the event of preliminaries, or after buy)

You can likewise characterize the quantity of recharges for which associates will be appointed or keep up the commission pertinent for all membership restorations (renewal).

If you can set the partner commission to zero, subsidiaries will not get any commissions or warnings for clients' orders. Undispatched requests won't be enlisted in the subsidiary reports; however, they are followed in the "Merchant Control Panel" as requests created by affiliates.

4. Terms and Conditions.

Characterize your Terms and Conditions concerning the marketing of affiliate's practices that members ought to hold fast to. Empower the "Add custom terms and conditions" choice and utilize the supervisor to embed and organize the terms and conditions. Snap Save settings when you are set, and your associates will get the terms and conditions when they demand another association. The terms & conditions are dependent upon consistency endorsement, following a survey made by 2Checkout. When we endorse or reject the custom terms & conditions, you'll get an email notification. Organization strategically pitching concession controls the impetuses you offer for your items when utilized as strategically pitching alternatives by different traders (which go about as your associates, in this specific case).

3.3 Discounts

Inside the commission list, you can permit the allocated associates to create rebate coupons from their bonuses and determine the most extreme sum for the concession. You empower associates to control the cost of your contributions inside a predetermined reach and furnish expected clients with better arrangements. The value distinction is deducted from the associate commission. This sort of showcasing is ideal for offshoots running coupon/limits situated sites. Permit Affiliates the opportunity to offer limits from their edge. This can help support transformation rates on their part.

3.4 Credit affiliates for renewals

The alternative to credit associates for renewals permits you to credit 2Checkout associates that initially alluded a deal with their bonus for renewals of the license of the equivalent products. The commission for renewal of the license will be equivalent to the first deal. Empower this choice if you sell programming items that help renewals of license items.

Chapter: 4 Compensation Methods for affiliate Marketing?

Compensation methods are existing in so many types of online marketing, including affiliate marketing. There are different types of compensation methods, each method of compensation pays significantly and has a specific potential profit. What is the best one for you?

In between merchant and affiliate, the major thing is the compensation method they will have to settle on, and they will be used. For this plan, merchants normally provide one compensation method, although some of them which offer multiple. An affiliate will select the affiliate method that is more likely to be successful and therefore earn the highest return if there is an option. The merchants' compensation method's preference is defined by the sort of conversions that they choose to obtain through the affiliate network. Both merchants and affiliates can take beneficial about multiple compensation methods and what they represent.

- Pay-Per-Click

- Pay-Per-Impression or Pay-Per-View

- Pay-Per-Lead

- Pay-Per-Sale

- Two-Tier Affiliate Programs

4.1 Pay-Per-Click (PPC)

Pay-Per-Click can be used only for bloggers or those who have high traffic websites. To get him to your website, the reader has to click on links, and any time this happens, the writer earns a commission. No transactions need to be made; you just pay for the traffic contributing to new buyers, ideally. As a business, you may decline to pay the writer if you believe they are clicking the link themselves or by automatic strategies that do not give you new clients.

4.2 Pay-Per-Impression or Pay-Per-View

This method is also known as Pay-Per-View. Pay-Per-Impression is a compensation method that pays depend on the number of views or impressions that an ad receives. This is abbreviated CPM from the advertiser's point of view, which stands for cost-per-mille or cost-per-thousand-impressions. This method is mostly used to show advertisements, video ads, text ads and so on.

4.3 Pay-Per-Lead (PPL)

Pay-Per-Lead is a challenging method, compensates the affiliate depending on conversion of leads. Affiliate must persuade the user to access merchant's website and complete the desired action, either filling out a contact request, subscribing to a newsletter, signing up for a product preview, or uploading files or applications.

4.4 Pay-Per-Sale (PPS)

This compensation method is the most commonly used. In this method, the merchant owes the affiliate a percentage of the product's selling price until the customer buys the product.

4.5 Two-Tier Affiliate Programs

An underlying affiliate network is managed by the affiliate marketer and earns commissions on both its referrals and those from its network. Such kind of affiliate program allows multi-level marketing. Organizations may implement a mixture of affiliate program types. For instance, through its Amazon Associates affiliate marketing scheme, Amazon utilizes both pay-per-action and pay-per-click for sales and leads Amazon to have a Amazon influencer program.

Chapter: 5 Building traffic and Cashing in on the customers.

Ask a marketer or company executive what they will want most in the future, and they would undoubtedly answer you "more customers." What really occurs on the wish list of a business after customers? Further traffic to their web. There are several aspects in which the website will boost traffic,

5.1 Get Social

It's not enough to generate good content, and you need to be proactive, trusting that people can find it. One of the simplest ways to improve the traffic to a website is to utilize social networking platforms for advertising your content. For fast, snappy (tempting) connections, the best is Twitter, while promotion of Google+ will help your site appear in the customized search results & tends to be very successful in B2B niches. If you are a B2C product company with image-heavy social sites like Pinterest & Instagram, you may search well traction.

5.2 Mixing It Up

For content marketing effectiveness, there is no magic formula, considering what others might have you believe. For this cause, change the material's length and style to make it as attractive to multiple types of readers as possible. For maximum impact, intersperse shorter, infographics, data-driven pieces and news-based blog posts with long-form content as well as video.

5.3 Target Long-Tail Keywords

Did you cover your high-intent keywords and common keyword bases? Then it's time for long-tail keyword targeting, too. A lot of site searches search for long-tail keywords, implying that you're losing out whether you're not targeting them as part of your paying quest or SEO efforts.

5.4 Inviting Others for Guest Blogging on Your Site

Blogging for guests is a two-way route. Invite users in your niche to comment on your own platform, in addition to posting content to other sites. They would probably share and link to their guest blog, which may attract fresh readers to your website. Only make sure you just upload high-quality, original content with no spammy links, because on low-quality guest blogging, Google cracks way down.

5.5 Make Sure Your Site is Fast

Have you found yourself struggling ever to launch a website for 30 seconds? And nor did me. And bounce rate will be very high if the web takes much longer to launch. Making sure the pages, including picture file sizes, web layout and third-party plugin features, are technically configured as practicable. The quicker it loads on your web, the easier.

5.6 Make Sure Your Site is Responsive

Long gone are the days when internet searching was performed solely on laptop PCs. Today, more users use mobile devices to navigate the internet than ever before, and if you push your visitors to scroll and navigate through the page, you're effectively advising them to go elsewhere. You will need to ensure that it is available and conveniently viewable across various platforms, like smaller smartphones, even though you have a basic website.

5.7 Pay Attention to On-Page SEO

Consider that SEO's dead? Again, remember. It is still a worthwhile and important practice for optimizing the content for search engines. Are you making the most of the Alt Text image? Are you creating links to fresh content internally? How regarding meta's definition? On-page SEO optimization does not have to take ages, and it might really improve the organic traffic.

5.8 Examine Your Analytics Data

Google Analytics is an important collection of knowledge, from the most famous sites to visitor demographics, on just about every possible web component. Keep a close watch on your details from Analytics and use this knowledge to advise your strategy for marketing and material. Pay attention to what the most famous blogs and sites are. To see who from where & when a website's traffic is coming, inspect the user info.

5.9 Be Active on the Social Media Platforms

It isn't enough to share content only via social channels-you still need to engage actively in the community. Got an account on Twitter?

Then interact with related hashtags in community conversations. Is your viewer leaving your Facebook updates with comments? Answer questions and connect the readers about them. Using social media as it was planned and engaging with your followers, the best thing to shut people down is using social media as a broadcast platform.

5.10 Incorporate Video into Your Content

Text-based content is all fine and, but **the** video is **a** more powerful tool, even engaging new visitors and having the website more immersive. Research indicates that the preservation of data is dramatically greater for visual content than for text, which implies that video marketing is an ideal opportunity to attract and retain your viewers' interest and, in the meantime, increase traffic to your website.

5.11 Research the Competition

You are at a massive disadvantage if you haven't used tools like BuzzSumo to find out what your opponents are up to. These programs aggregate the social success of individual websites and posts that can provide you with an at-a-glance view of what concerns connect with readers and, most importantly, make social media rounds.

To get attention to your page, figure out what people read (and talking about), and imitate that kind of material.

5.12 Appear on podcasts

A podcast has been listened to by 44 percent of the US community. Podcasts have been one of the hottest marketing outlets because of that. Brands such as Drift are flocking to the podcast game and making their own models. But it is **a** tedious job to make a podcast. You'll need tools, expertise for editing, visitors, etc. And it doesn't seem like a smart idea to dive right into setting up one if you have **few** resources.

5.13 Make Yourself Heard in Comment Sections

You probably regularly visit at least a few important places to your business, so why not enter the conversation? Commenting does not offer an instant boost to referral traffic instantly but getting a reputation for yourself is a fantastic way to get your name out there by providing informative, thought-provoking comments on business blogs and pages, which can then contribute to attracting more traffic to your own platform. Note that you can engage with other individuals in your niche, not dropping spam links to random websites, as guest hosting, content, and relevance are essential.

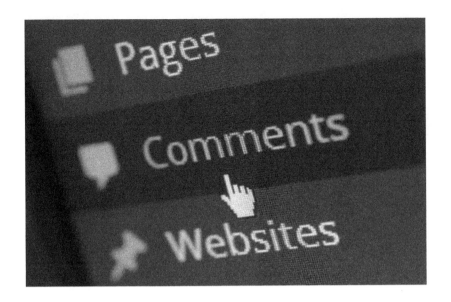

5.14 Enhance Sense of Community

Many People like to talk their minds & weigh in on issues they are strongly about, so it is right chance to start a dialogue and boost traffic to your page to create a community on your site. Use third-party solutions, such as Facebook comments, to introduce a comprehensive commenting platform or build a website to ask some questions. However, do not hesitate in managing the culture to guarantee that certain decorum needs are met.

5.15 Attend Conferences

No matter which business you doing, the chances are that there would be at least one or two big conventions and conferences important to your business. It is a smart thing to visit these events; it is much better to talk to them. An outstanding way to develop yourself as a thought leader in your field and achieve significant exposure to your web is also a halfway good speaking engagement.

Chapter: 6 Additional tips on how to earn money as an affiliate

Following are the tips on how to earn money as an affiliate.

6.1 Choose More Attractive Products

Everything promoting by registering with various affiliate programs will be a definite error. You can't concentrate intensely on each of them, and that will be a failure as a result. Only advertise a few items which are special, valuable or can hit broad masses, instead of promoting everything. To earn money as an affiliate, you need to understand customer demands and expectations and place your items accordingly.

6.2 Review Sites for Your Affiliate Program

Eighty-four percent of customers trust reviews as well as their friends, according to Inc, determine the value of finding a trustworthy review site for your affiliate program or website. Three fundamental principles to remember when evaluating if a review platform for your affiliate program is trustworthy are mentioned below:

- **Research the Review Site**

Researching comments on a review forum can help to evaluate the degree of faith in their views. Since they won't have as much reputation as existing reviewers, be careful of "new review sites." Finally, make sure all other similar product articles are read.

- **Watch out for Similar Wording in Reviews**

This may indicate that the review websites are being reimbursed for their ratings, leading to a skewed evaluation for an affiliate partner. Read other reviews to recognize if this is a trend.

- **Ignore Drastic Review Sites.**

If a review forum consistently posts an enormous amount of favorable or unfavorable feedback, conducting further investigation on the site can be a strong predictor. The site could have incentives to publish dramatic feedback that may lead to skewed results in particular.

6.3 Stay Consistent

To improve and see your efforts' benefits, you need to remain loyal to affiliate marketing long enough. It's not simple. To see things out to a satisfying result is a question of self-control and patience.

Ideally, out of the affiliate marketing tactics, build a daily routine. If you run advertisements, make monitoring your data, logging and ads a routine. Make it a routine to compose an article whenever you write a blog. Do something long enough to make it sound incorrect not to do it! For a pattern to become part of the routine, it normally takes around one month.

Make your affiliate business a focus, and this would benefit you for the longer term. Compile a list of the reasons that you do this as well. When you're not feeling like it, this can benefit - which will certainly happen.

6.4 Do not rush

Affiliate marketing isn't a way to immediately get rich. During their first month or two, people imagine earning hundreds of thousands, which is not possible. You will need a couple of months before you start to see some money seeping in, and persons who get compensated early on are not only lucky; they are sure to put in a lot of hard work to make it possible.

People who have too big hopes for their earnings end up frustrated, and so, within a few months, they generally leave their efforts. So you have to stand with things if you have realistic goals.

Chapter: 7 Managing an Affiliate Business

There are the following rules that how to manage an affiliate business.

7.1 Have the best monitoring affiliate you can purchase or create.

As you'd have to pay either a fixed dollar value per transaction or a proportion of overall revenue, verifying the source of each sale is important. Many businesses who promote affiliate offers have their own tracking programs to guarantee that consumers are monitored from the moment they see an advertisement on a vendor page for your brand, through the period when that consumer visits your e-commerce platform, and finally to the time that customer buys your product. You may need to purchase or create a straightforward framework that will manage all monitoring if you are handling the affiliate marketing network in-house.

Anyway, you must have your own monitoring scheme for affiliate marketing to match those incoming buyers on your e-commerce platform to a specific order. Getting strong monitoring records ensures that even if your business's revenue figures do not meet your partner suppliers' numbers, you will shield yourself from any discussions that may occur. Any fundamental details can come from Google Analytics e-commerce monitoring, but you also want to ask your backed developer or database administrator whether you can directly get the information from your sales management system.

7.2 Know how much you can spend per lead

Before you reach an agreement about how much you can invest in affiliate payments, you need to consider how much sales and profits you assume you will receive per client. That way, you will handle the needs of affiliates and also for yourself.

If you really are offering a tangible commodity, then to find profitability, use the expense of the item and sale price. In order to get overall unit revenues and a rise in income, the profit is what you would lose with affiliate fees. If you recognize your own profit and your planned return rate, early preparation will hold your margin stable even at elevated revenue speed.

If you offer a subscription plan, you must know how long the typical user would be subscribing and also how much monthly the subscriber will cost. That knowledge will have a higher overall sum you can invest per client while retaining profitability. The downside being that it will take a few months to make back what you spent on the client if what you pay per client is much more than a single month's subscription.

7.3 Realize where your affiliate partners are advertising

You may already be investing in paying search ads, or on certain pages, you may have digital advertising offers. Affiliate advertisement networks that are not tightly controlled might begin to negotiate with you about your own phrases, intellectual property rights, and logos. They may be eligible to get their search engine ranking elevated than your business promotion site, based on how they support you. This suggests that you could end up having to pay for a deal that should have been free for an unlimited quest. It's important to set some basic affiliate management guidelines for each affiliate marketer where they can advertise because it's like hiring a corporation to compete for themselves because that ensures you will just have to pay for the cheaper choice. A smart idea to do is still ask for evidence such as screenshots of your position from each new affiliate. Understand what sorts of positioning you have on their channels and understand what instruments they use. In order to control how they utilize your advertisement materials more efficiently; you can also inquire what demographic group they are reaching for your items.

7.4 Measure results on a daily basis

Even with a partnership with a good affiliate marketing associate, there may be issues with their information like data at times, and it's very necessary to equate their data with your monitoring data. Not all partnership pages are as open or very well managed as they can be, and it's useful to discover whether the affiliate network partner's sales information has positive or negative patterns.

On a regular Wednesday, if one of your associates ranges from 10 transactions per day to 1,000 sales, you must first verify whether anything appears right or if there are any errors in the data. If it's a true transition, see if those new buyers are performing like ten transactions per day in the longer term. If it seems lucrative, then open up the budget to see if you can repeat the performance again by making 10,000 revenue from them.

It would be more appropriated to stop it instead of struggling with 3,000 nonprofitable clients by Friday and 5,000 by Monday if those latest thousand-odd transactions sound like customers that are not the same standard as the usual ten regulars.

7.5 Build healthy relations

In Affiliate Marketing, there are several aspects of honesty. Be sure that you will pay in a timely way as a consumer of these facilities. Learn to understand how much you should invest with your management partners in financing (or whoever is operating finance). Set out fair payment conditions, such as net 30 versus all pre-paid, and ensure that the affiliates you deal with will comply with the timeline.

Spend time developing the right collaborators in the program and reducing deadweight affiliates that are not productive. It's really convenient for an affiliate to guarantee performance or lead number. Still, it's far tougher for them to offer volume to such buyers, and this is why you want to become the buyer they want to interact with in the longer term. It's not a run, but a race.

Chapter: 8 Affiliate Marketers Mistakes

Why do most Bloggers Fail in Affiliate Marketing?

The reality is that most blogs at Affiliate Marketing struggle badly.

8.1 Some bloggers believe they really grasp the concept of affiliate marketing well.

This is one of the strangest explanations why bloggers with affiliate marketing struggle to increase revenue. When you believe you know something completely, you eliminate the possibility of learning new information. The Internet is full of free affiliate marketing deals, but many of them are outdated. (written in 2012 or earlier!) Those items that succeeded a few years back have very little effect on today's social media marketing environment. We must remain accessible to different things and respond to improvements by learning to succeed in today's online marketing environment. Check for the finest training that you can get, ask for advice, and purchase it! You would expect to see a suggestion for an Affiliate Marketing tool at this point in an article, but we don't do it here since, as we mentioned, goods and strategies change constantly, and what we prescribe today may not be acceptable in the next couple of years. However, if you are really interested in Internet Marketing, we would propose a Facebook Community that everybody can enter, that is "Internet Marketing Super Mates."

It's not all about affiliate marketing; there are tons of tips on anything relating to digital marketing and daily updates with a real abundance of talent. Good bloggers and associates are still discovering, never believing that they know all!

8.2 They promote commodities for money only

This is the Negative Truth of affiliate marketing-it is ethically wrong to promote any item just for the sake of commissions. Test any product you advertise yourself, start with, and ask yourself, will I purchase it? Now, if you have discovered a product that you'd like to promote, how can you be sure that your audience would like to know about it? To start with, you could do some beneficial market surveys by posting stories on your blogging website.

- Try identifying the most widely shared articles on your website.

- Mark the blogs with the largest amount of responses.

- Classify the most commonly related posts.

- Classify the posts that fuel the search engines for the most searches.

Of course, through running a questionnaire on your blog, you can also discover what your audiences want and need. The more significant the commodity you advertise, the greater your chances of profits and commissions being produced.

8.3 They do not invest in the essential tools

Without spending on the correct instruments, there is no enterprise you can effectively do online. You need to buy many tools for bloggers who are keen to excel in affiliate marketing to positively impact your revenues. Some of these instruments include;

- Premium Rapid Pace Hosting Service

- Competent quick theme launching

- Premium extensions for product analysis enabling user-generated feedback

- Domination Popup

- SEO software, such as modules like Yoast.

Also, very importantly, they don't stay up to speed with the marketplace's shifts. Technology, SEO, and social networking are evolving all the time. Please realize that six months from now, what works now will function differently.

8.4 They have minor knowledge of the items they promote

This one is a tight friendship, just for the profits, to sell a commodity! How would you ever sell something efficiently without understanding the item? Will you purchase a vehicle from a dealer who didn't own a car? This is the perfect way to earn extra revenue with an affiliate product. When you support a commodity that you use, you would be endorsing it from a pleased consumer's point of view. You would be able to show how this has benefited you out. Know that readers enjoy 'stories,' and one of the best persuasive tactics is telling how you become infatuated with this.

There's One More Tip: Most manufacturing companies can create a promotional letter, efficiently written by a trained copywriter, but note, individuals purchase from individuals, so it is advised to include your own description (video is good) while marketing a product. By just saying 'check this out,' you give people a justification why they must check this product out.

8.5 They only do what other people do

You have to distinguish between yourself and other affiliates; only then will you be able to make extra money. So many members just end up copy-pasting - don't do something like that! Be an inventor and come up with a viewpoint that others don't have. Have you discovered an advantage that others don't have? It may even be only an advantage for you and some others, but insert that benefits and opportunities that other people will see as an advantage as well. Besides, and this is essential, add your tale about why you got started with this item. Recently, the great achievement story of a mother who initiated online purely to make enough money for her daughter to pay for horse riding lessons. Of course, this was aimed at the Newcomer Marketer, and it also had that all significant feeling of 'feeling content.' Other stuff you can do. For example, => For your audience, add a special reward Make a special promo code from the author of the product => => Get an author's co-branded sales page Successful affiliates are inventors who always seek to create quality to the offer, either in terms of a bonus prize or, in my view reveal a perspective or tactic that nobody else talks about.

8.6 They lack Strategies

Now, point 5 above is strongly connected to this point. When you use your mind as an associate writer, marketing tactics that most people lack, you will still come up with them. Currently, most affiliate marketing sites allow retailers to produce their affiliates with special discount codes. The best thing is that most manufacturers are happy for you to get a special code at any moment. You should still negotiate exclusive offers with your subscribers with this in mind. One of the things that were done some time ago that produced some insane sales is that a product-focused discussion with a retailer is scheduled on the blog. This helped me to frame questions that prompted suitable responses to generate further sales. In order to generate more affiliate revenue, you must constantly dream about some innovative tactics and do it differently.

8.7 They do feature-based reviews

WIIFM = What's in It for Me? This is one of the questions that Customers want to know about. But too many product reports rely on the Rewards instead of the Functionality. People may not want to acquire a quarter-inch drill, as Theodore Levitt claimed. "they want to purchase quarter-inched hole!" And Mr. Levitt told that "Kodak sells movies, but they do not advertise movies; they do advertise memories," for those of us old enough to remember. Get it? Don't dwell on the characteristics; focus on the advantages! Know the Features Speak; Advantages Sell The raison d'être of every affiliate product you support should be to fix a dilemma. If the problem-solving potential is not highlighted in the analysis, the point of the product is absent!

8.8 They neglect SEO

For most writers, SEO is the sole greatest site of paid advertising without massive budgets. Yeah, Social Networking still functions, but SEO gives the most focused visitors to my knowledge. Why should SEO not be neglected? => Do analysis on keywords when conducting an associate product evaluation => Aim the proper keyword for purchasing in your analysis articles => Do OnPage SEO correctly on your product analysis articles => Encourage a media platforms product analysis article to attract likes, tweets and comments. => Build backlink profile to articles for the product review => Quest for the best

SEO Techniques The more visits you receive from web pages on your review posts, the more money you can produce. It is no more about attempting to trick search engines (Black Hat) but about partnering with search engines to include knowledge in the best available way. Note that SEO evolves all the time. Be sure to verify out Schema.org for a series of expandable frameworks on this topic that enable web users to insert standardized data for search engine use on their web pages. It's the latest SEO!

8.9 They do not promote monthly payment items (and commissions).

Put clearly, you have an option to endorse a One-Payment offer or a product that needs a monthly payment while marketing goods (Software or membership usually). Of course, you can have a combination of both, but it is preferred to encourage periodic payments wherever possible, which pay me profits over the duration of the recurring payment. Payments are typically once a month; however, extension plans are often paid out periodically or annually. To receive recurring permits, identify subscription places that have partner services in your niche and work on introducing them to your audience. There are also tech and hosting businesses that pay out annual fees.

8.10 They do not have a targeted list.

In my early stages of blogging, one of the errors made by me was that my journal began without creating a list. "The money is on the list," it's usually said, and that's valid to a degree. But if the list is incorrectly made, you would never see any cash from it. Something not discussed often is: Not all the customers are similar or equal. Many subscribers are more inclined to purchase from you than others simply because of how they discovered you. Standard, in other words, typically beats quantity. It is seen writers are inclined to purchase lists or borrow them; however, it should be stopped.

8.11 They do not focus on Content and Targeted traffic.

For Affiliate Marketing to work, you need =>quality material = Directed audience. As a content writer and an affiliate marketer, it matters more than anything else. Still, a lot of blogs focus on items like style and colors of the font and size, while great content and related search engine traffic should still be their real targets. If you have no material that draws viewers who subscribe to your list, there is no use in creating the greatest theme and being housed on the must-robust server on planet Earth.

One Ultimate Idea. You should always train to thrive as an affiliate marketer, and this website has loads of opportunities for that. This page has plenty of links about how to create interactive content and content that is circulated, in addition to links on list creation and general blogging. To your success in Affiliate Marketing.

8.12 Lack of Patience

You should know that it takes 2-3 years for most established small companies to make a profit; how can we expect an affiliate corporation to generate a profit in a very little time span? Fortunately, costs are usually relatively minimal for affiliate advertisers. This ensures it is possible to see profitability quicker than other firms. But before hoping to see a profit, you must intend to serve for 6 to 12 months without seeing a penny. You can trust me or trust all the "get rich quick" experts out there. What I'm saying you may not be what you'd like to learn, but you must be capable of working for free in order to thrive. Later on, you can be paid with a deferred salary for some years. In the long-run, it is a simple transaction. I wrote a lot more comprehensive post about how long it might take to become a full-time marketer for affiliates.

8.13 Refusing to invest and reinvest in their business

In our community, it is totally reasonable to waste $30 on a movie and popcorn or to drop $6 on a single ounce of beer at the pub, but it is simply too much to spend in a corporation that would yield deferred sales on a vehicle for years. I mean, think!? The costs are higher when you are planning to start a proper business. When you're an affiliate marketer, holding your costs below $100 / mo. is really feasible. And think about it, how many enterprise models actually operate where the costs can be held below $100 a month? It's a great opportunity to make money online, so be ready to at least spend a small sum per month on developing your business. What would you do when you receive the first $500 from your affiliate marketing business? Will you want to save it? Will you pay any personal loans?   Will you buy a fun new toy for your son, or taking a weekend trip? Pause for a second! I re-invested my income from the moment I got my first $8 in affiliate fees (you can read the tale here). I re-invested 100 percent of my earnings for the first few months. I'm still re-investing my profits these days, but it's a lot less than before. It's all right to have some of your earnings for yourself. You've won it! But note, the more you invest in your business, the faster you can evolve, and the more you can increase the number of promotions you receive every day.

Chapter: 9 Advantages of Affiliate Marketing

Starting an online business is becoming easier these days, but it is very difficult to manage and make the most of it. While affiliate marketing has its drawbacks, it can give you a good way to earn at the end of the day.

So, before beginning affiliate marketing, carefully review the site, its advantages, disadvantages, and then choose your decision. If it really all functions well, you should give it a chance.

1. Easy to Start

This is perhaps the most reasonable component in this platform's decision. Every one of affiliate marketing's facilities proves that this is the perfect way to start your business. To complete the entire process when beginning with the platform, you only need to follow some simple steps.

2. Easy to Earn

The affiliate marketing scheme provides an easy way to generate additional revenue sources for website publishers and owners. Merchant commodity advertisement banners produce immediate sales where they earn a profit.

3. Time-Saving

Without spending precious time, the merchant can gain more customers.

4. Broad Area

Merchants are getting a broad area to promote their goods and services, resulting in more sales and customers.

5. Promote Complimentary Products

In affiliate marketing, apart from the primary items, you may have opportunities to sell complementary items as an affiliate. It also enhances the chance to grow your income.

6. Merchant responsibility

As the merchant manages everything in affiliate marketing, the affiliate does not have to care about consumer service, bookkeeping, and e-commerce-related headaches; all the affiliate has to do is advertise and resell the product.

7. Work from anywhere

An affiliate marketer loves the privilege of becoming his own manager and operating on his own time. He may only operate for a couple of hours or so to earn 24/7 revenue anywhere he might be in the world.

8. Retain Current Job

An affiliate marketer may also retain his current job or business and have the affiliate's marketing profits to complement his financial status. With a laptop and internet access, even though enjoying a vacation, anyone can function virtually everywhere.

9. No Travelling

They do not have to go all the way to the merchant's shop or retailer for customers to physically purchase the goods or engage a service provider's services.

Chapter: 10 Disadvantages of Affiliate Marketing

These are some drawbacks that do not promote in affiliate marketing.

1. Inaccurate Ads

To get sales commissions, the affiliates may participate in inaccurate and defamatory ads. Disreputable affiliates may make assertions and commitments, which are completely false or highly unrealistic, about the goods and services. In situations like this, complaints are usually received by the merchant and all potential customers are lost.

2. False Advertisement

False ads, illegal usage of trademarks, brands, or products are also present.

3. Uncertainty

Opportunities present threats, and the same issue occurs in the promotion of affiliates. There is no guarantee that the revenue can meet a certain amount if well-planned strategies are not set and followed. To extract the maximum output, you have to provide your utmost, but you can't promise that your income would be a definite amount.

Every now and then, the affiliate revenue can fluctuate. If a large spectrum of customers can rise, it can be said that you can estimate an average flow of revenue.

4. Big Competition

Promoting any item in this dynamic marketplace is an extremely tough job. If you chose some item to advertise your site, several people are already doing the same while you are planning for it.

So, it's really hard to get or get the focus of the appropriate person.

5. Select the right Item/Product

It's still a challenging job to make it happen when selecting the best item from a lot of items. You will find a lot of items on the market for affiliate marketing. So before finding the best item that might suit you, make sure to do the right homework.

6. Highjack Links

Link hijackers are possible to hijack affiliate links and instead get paid for the revenues.

Chapter 11: Nine great ways to generate traffic for your affiliate offers

You are not the only one if you fail to get visitors to your associate offerings.

63 % of all the organizations claim that generating leads and traffic is one of the leading marketing challenges.

The advertiser has already developed the service or product and the affiliate scheme of affiliate marketing and provided the requisite resources and creatives to help promote their offering. The critical difficulty that publishers face is to create traffic through an affiliate connection to these affiliate deals, which equates to further traffic to the advertiser's website. Ideally, this adds to further conversions and better income. Therefore, it must be at the forefront of publishers' list of goals to attract traffic.

We also researched some of its most powerful forms in which publishers can create traffic for certain associate deals and share our top nine strategies below.

1. Paid online advertising

Publicizing is the backbone of lead creation. Regardless of whether you decide to do web-based media campaigns, paid inquiry, show publicizing, or remarketing, it's an attempted and tried the technique to direct people to your associate links.

One of the upsides of utilizing paid lead producing procedures is that individuals who click on your connections are generally high up in the purchasing cycle and are consequently prepared to buy. Nevertheless, you require to adjust the expense of your ads with the commission you get per deal. On the off chance that every promotion change costs $50 and the commission per deal is $40, it does not merit seeking after this type of lead creation.

2. YouTube

YouTube is 2nd largest search engine on the web, with around three billion perspectives each day. Accordingly, it is advantageous for you to begin your channel to advance your offers. Add an intriguing video that identifies with your offer, at that point, incorporate a convincing source of inspiration that connects to your offshoot item. Make a point to likewise put your source of inspiration connection or markdown code inside the portrayal box, with a short depiction of your video. Additionally, use your video add an Overlay, which is a little box that stays on the video all through with your CTA on it.

Try not to limit to YouTube only as different video channels are there, such as Vimeo, which can be utilized to acceptable impact. Nonetheless, one of the burdens of video advancement is it requires some investment and exertion to create a great substance that will pull in a reliable crowd. On the addition to side, incredible recordings can become a web sensation and raise countless watchers rapidly.

Furthermore, when advancing subsidiary proposals via online media, make sure to follow the consistency and divulgence rules plot by the FTC for utilizing associate links.

3. Social media

In the event that your crowd is hanging out via social media, at that point, you and your associate's offers should be there as well. You can utilize social media from various perspectives, including:

- Participating in networks with a requirement for your item. However, it's significant not to elevate to assemble connections by addressing questions and drawing in with the local area. In the event that you are useful, your perusers will tap on your name to discover more about you. Ensure your profile interfaces back to your site, and your associate offers. Searching for a spot to begin? Join our special Awin for Bloggers Facebook gathering.

- Sharing your blog material, either as sponsored blogs or on your page, with links to your offer.

- Running a publicizing effort, utilizing social media advertising.

You can likewise utilize social media to distribute long articles, which connect to your offers. Great spots to distribute incorporate stages, such as Medium, Udemy, Reddit, LinkedIn, and SlideShare. Readership of these locales is high, and if your substance is applicable and accessible, it could get you before a large number of new individuals.

Once more, when utilizing associate connections via social media, ensure you're following the consistency and divulgence rules delineated by the FTC.

4. Blog posts

Blog entries are an extraordinary method to share associate connections. On the off chance that you have a functioning readership, your crowd will, as of now, be warm to your audits and guidance. Make a point not to utilize your blog entries as direct mail advertisements; the substance must offer some incentive to the peruser. Your subsidiary connections ought to sit normally inside the theme. Formula sites utilize this to great impact. As they talk about the strategy to follow to make the dish, formula online journals depict the devices required for the work, utilizing member connects to the business page of the thing being referred to.

Another technique for utilizing your blog entries to elevate member joins is to answer your perusers' remarks and utilize your subsidiary connections in the answers. In the event that the item you are elevating is identified with the appropriate response, it doesn't appear as though an attempt to close the deal; however, an answer for the peruser's concern. Be cautious about doing this on others' sites as it might appear to be spam.

Evergreen alludes to content that stays significant for a long time to come and could incorporate how-to guides, best practices, or tips and deceives. These sorts of articles are perused and alluded to again and again. Although you may need to revive them sometimes, the data stays pertinent. This implies you can reveal this substance to another crowd now and then and uncover your offshoot connects each time you do as such.

5. Guest blogging

Notwithstanding building your image's blog, the strategy of visitor writing for a blog is a reliable technique for creating traffic that has stood the trial of time. There are two distinct perspectives to visitor contributing to a blog:

- Guest blog on notable destinations that fit your specialty. Offer incredible and pertinent substance, and whenever acknowledged onto different sites, it will open you to a different crowd. Ensure your profile and your byline connection to your offshoot offers and your site. Your offshoot showcasing substance must be identified with the visitor blog and helpful to the new likely readership.

- Accept visitor bloggers on your site. Distribute content from different journalists, and they will share and connect their article, which will, thus, uncover your site (and associate offers) to new crowds.

6. Email

Marketing through email is as yet fit as a fiddle, with 64% of organizations trusting it is the best advertising technique they have, with an expected ROI of 3800%. Along these lines, ensure you don't disregard it in light of some fresher, additional energizing strategies.

You first need to construct a rundown, that you must do through giving a free offer - like sharing a report, digital book, or online class - and utilizing a structure to catch email address (ensuring, in the event that you are advertising in the EU, to follow GDPR). While messaging your rundown, you should be mindful of giving them valuable, pertinent substance. Else, they will rapidly withdraw.

Associate connections can be utilized to acceptable impact in messages, either as a feature of the body text or in the mark. Likewise, it is completely worth advancing associate items straightforwardly in messages, as long as you offset it out with significant and valuable substance. In the event that conceivable, portion your messages, so the fitting subsidiary connections go to the correct crowd.

7. Product reviews

The online crowd is impacted by others' perspectives on an item and frequently investigates for tributes and surveys prior to purchasing. It's assessed that 90% of potential purchasers will peruse online surveys before visiting the site and settling on a purchasing choice, with 88% believing them however much they would if a companion suggested an item.

For distributors who have developed a steadfast crowd, these insights are uplifting news. On the off chance that you compose fair and unprejudiced surveys about items identified with your specialty, your crowd will see these audits as a reliable proposal. When you have an item or administration to elevate that is attached to your member-promoting endeavors, compose an audit. In the event that you have decided to advance the item, it is significant that you have confidence in it and prescribe it since you need to help your crowd. This way, you will want to compose a straightforward and genuine survey while including your partner connect. The audit should be positive, however fair, and ought not to transform into a direct mail advertisement.

Ensure when utilizing subsidiary connections in item surveys to follow the FTC's consistency and exposure rules plot.

8. Quora

Quora is an inquiries site, giving a stage to clients to ask anything they desire. Specialists at that point offer direction and guidance on the topic. Albeit direct associate connections are not permitted, you can get a connection to a site or a blog entry if it gives more data on the appropriate response you are giving. Ensure the site you send individuals to contains content with your subsidiary connection.

Once more, when utilizing Quora, you should truly hope to give a legitimate answer and help the individual present the inquiry. Solid counsel will be perused and shared, while answers simply attempting to seal the deal will get disapproval.

9. A search engine optimized website

Your site is the introducing brand for your associate connections and should be found by shoppers intrigued by your specialty. Making your substance simple for web indexes to find your website is significant, as it will help rank your webpage higher up on ventures and drive more natural traffic to your subsidiary offers.

Each page ought to have an elegantly composed meta depiction, H1/H2 labels meta title, and picture alt labels. Examination the catchphrases for your specialty and associate offers, and add a watchword for every page pertinent to your offers. Guaranteeing it is in the title and substance as normally as expected, without catchphrase stuffing, can likewise assist with the look. Additionally, work on accomplishing backlinks by getting your substance shared via online media or different sites and incorporate inward and outer connections inside your substance.

In the process that the picked subject is too specialized, you may not get the degree of traffic you need to change your perusers into taps on your subsidiary connections. Do some examination on the number of others are selling comparable items by utilizing the Google search bar. Google will immediately disclose the number of results they have found and can help educate the keywords you use to web crawler enhance your website.

What techniques you decide to produce traffic will rely on your inclinations, offers, and industry. Numerous advertisers join a combination of organic and paid sources. Whichever strategies you like to use to create traffic to your offshoot offers, consistency is vital. Indeed, even with paid traffic, the more you keep up your missions, the better they will perform. Keep with it, and traffic will come in your direction.

Chapter 12: Start with Your Site Structure

The better your site structure, the better your opportunity of positioning higher in the web crawlers. Each site has some "structure." It may be a thorough and smoothed-out design, or it could be a disarranged mix of pages. In the event that you are deliberate and cautious with this site structure, you'll make a site that accomplishes search greatness.

The tips beneath will help you make a site that bids to clients, gets crept and ordered by insects, and conveys the best SERP postings and rankings conceivable.

12.1 Why structure matters

Since many people have worked with a huge number of clients over several years, they have, in reality, been stunned by how much the format of the web is hard to remember. Or It's among the most basic parts of SEO achievement of a stage, on the one side. Yet, in actuality, a few website admins proprietors acknowledge what it involves getting a webpage design that helps SEO.

There's a couple of clarifications on why the web format is so basic and how to fabricate your SEO-accommodating web composition.

When you remove the tones, textual styles, kerning, illustrations, pictures, and void area, great site configuration is truly about incredible construction.

12.2 Site structure means great user experience.

The human brain aches for intellectual balance — having the option to assemble pieces consistently, discovering things where they're normal, and finding what they are looking for. In this way, a solid and sensible site structure is psychologically fulfilling to clients.

As you probably are aware, the seriously engaging your site to clients, the engaging it is to web crawlers. The algorithm of Google utilizes data from searchers to categories your website. If your website has week CTRs and abides time, it won't perform well in SERPs. Paradoxically, when a client finds a website that clients like — for example, the website with extraordinary construction — they do not skip & they remain longer. An exact website structure can lessen bob rate and abide time; the two of these will prompt enhanced rankings.

12.3 A site structure provides your site with site links.

Website links are a posting design in SERPs that show your website's principal page alongside a few inside links sunken underneath. You have observed them previously.

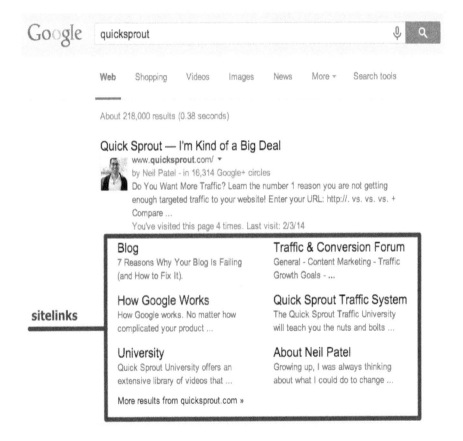

Site links are a gigantic SEO advantage. They increment the traversability of your site, guide clients toward the most pertinent data, increment the reputation of your brand, improve the trust of clients, assist you with overwhelming

SERPs, clickthrough rate increment, and conversion funnel shortening. Fundamentally, site links are magnificent.

In any case, how would you approach site links? You do not just go to "Google Search Console" and fill in a couple of fields on the structure. You cannot give a site link demand. The algorithm of Google naturally grants sites with site links. Also, they also dependent on extraordinary site structure.

In the event that you have a weak site structure, your site won't ever get site links. The site links' absence could be appraising your site focused on traffic, expanded conversions, and higher CTR.

12.4 Good structure means better crawling.

Web crawlers, just like Googlebot, slither the structure of the website. They will likely record the substance to restore it in list items. The greater your website structure, the simpler the crawlers can approach and record the substance.

Crawlers do not naturally find everything on the site. Google also concedes "[there're] pages on the site we might not... find,"/"URLs that might not be searchable by Google's ordinary crawling cycle." (That's one reason why sitemaps are essential.) Yet, crawlers will get a far simpler time getting to, creeping, ordering, and restoring the website's pages with a solid structure.

To summarize, your site's association makes you ready for SEO achievement. Indeed, it very well may be contended that without a decent website structure, you won't ever have SEO achievement. A solid website structure provides your website with a strong SEO establishment that will give you huge measures of search that is organic.

12.5 Six steps to creating a site structure

1. Plan out some hierarchy order before you build up your site.

In case you're beginning a site without any preparation, you're in an extraordinary situation to design out a website structure for the possible ideal SEO. Indeed, even prior to you begin making pages in the CMS, plan out the structure. You can achieve this using whiteboard, something similar to OmniGraffle or Visio, or most word processors and a spreadsheet program (Google Sheets, Excel).

A "hierarchy system" is just an approach to arranging your data — something basic and bodes well. Your order will likewise turn into your route and your site link structure, so all the things significant starts here.

For the most part, a hierarchy of site resembles this:

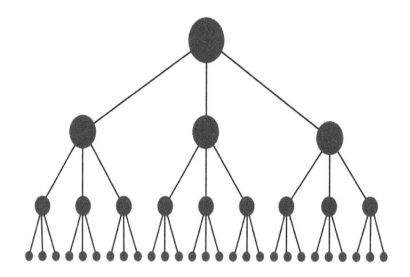

There are a couple of highlights of order that you should remember.

- Made your hierarchy legitimate. Don't overcomplicate or overthink this cycle. You need effortlessness, both for the good of your own and the simplicity of crawlers and clients. Every fundamental class ought to be remarkable and unmistakable. Each subcategory should identify with the fundamental class under which it is found by one way or another.

- Keep the number of primary classifications somewhere in the range of two to seven. Except if you're Amazon.com, you would prefer not to have an excessive number of primary classifications. There ought to be a couple of fundamental things. In the event that you have more than seven, you might need to reevaluate the association and pare this a piece down.

- Try to adjust the number of subcategories inside every class. Fundamentally, attempt to keep it roughly even. If one primary class has 14 subcategories while another fundamental classification has just 3 subcategories, this could be somewhat unequal.

A site chain of the hierarchy is the starting point for an incredible site structure.

2. Make a URL structure that follows your route chain of hierarchy.

The second primary component in creating a solid site structure is the structure of your URL. In the event that you've coherently thoroughly examined the chain of hierarchy, this must not be excessively troublesome. The structure of your URL follows your progressive hierarchy.

Thus, suppose your order of hierarchy resembles this:

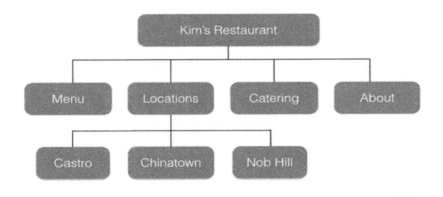

The structure of the URL for the Chinatown area would resemble this:

"www.kimsrestaurant.com/areas/chinatown"

The hierarchy of the site will coordinate your URL design. This implies that the URLs would have genuine words (without symbols) and fitting keywords inclusion.

3. Make your site route in CSS or HTML.

At the point when you make your route, keep the coding straightforward. CSS & HTML are your most secure methodology. Coding in Flash, AJAX, and JavaScript will restrict the crawler's capacity to cover the website's thoroughly examined route and chain of hierarchy.

4. Utilize a shallow profundity route structure.

Your route construction will follow the hierarchy of your site. Ensure the pages, particularly significant ones, are not covered excessively profoundly inside the site. Shallow websites work good, both from an ease of use and crawler point of view.

A shallow site (which is, one which needs 3 or less click to arrive at each page) is undeniably more ideal than a profound site (which needs protracted series of clicks to observe each page at your website).

5. Make a header that makes the list of your principle route pages.

Your upper header should show the list of your primary pages. Adding some other menu components separated from your fundamental classifications can become diverting and pointless. If you've planned a parallax site, make certain to give a tenacious header menu that shows through each stage of scrolling.

While menus of dropdown utilizing CSS impacts or vanishing menus may give an extraordinary or fascinating client experience, they don't improve SEO.

On the off chance that you've got a footer alongside menu links, make certain to copy your upper navigational menu's primary connections in the route of your footer menu. Altering the link's order or adding extra class postings will confound the client experience.

6. Build up a far-reaching inside the connecting structure.

Inside connecting puts meat at the bones of a consistent site chain of hierarchy. Three reasons why they are significant:

•They permit clients to explore a site.

•They help build up data hierarchy for a provided site.

•They assist in spreading connection juice (positioning force) around sites.

Every one of these is straightforwardly attached to making a very close and all-around coordinated site structure.

There is no convincing motivation to get jumbled with inward connecting. The essential thought is that each page on your site should connect to and some connection from another page on the site. Your route ought to achieve inward connecting to the subcategory pages and primary classifications; however, you ought to likewise ensure that leaf-level pages have inside connected too.

Inward connecting mentions to the web crawlers what pages are significant & how to arrive. The more interior connecting you've across whole pages, the improved.

The structure site is a result of a deliberate plan, cautious reasoning, and exact association. The best ideal opportunity to build up a solid structure of the site is to make your website. In any case, you are updating your site, and you must revise the plan and redesign a few navigational components to improve SEO's structures.

There are a ton of things to remember while upgrading your site for web indexes. The site's structure is quite possibly the most significant, yet perhaps the most ignored streamlining strategies. In the event that you have an incredible structure of the site, at that point, extraordinary SEO will follow.

Chapter 13: How to promote affiliate offers

Affiliate marketing assists you in incrementing commitment and income. However, it's not, at this point, barely enough to launch all these advertisements and expectations for progress.

Numerous brands and distributors have experienced declining natural reach on stages like Instagram and Facebook. Thus, bringing in cash through affiliate marketing is not just about as simple as making great content and organically distributing it. You require the correct promoting and effort methodologies to help you drive clients to your advertisements and accomplice distributers.

That is the reason we're separating the best nine affiliate marketing advancement strategies and methods to support your affiliate marketing and produce revenue:

- PPC
- SEO
- Reviews
- Webinars
- Email Marketing
- Coupons
- How-To Videos

- Blogging

- Social Media

Utilize the following affiliate marketing advancement techniques to receive views of your associate promotions.

1. PPC

PPC (Pay-per-click) publicizing includes dispatching advertisements, for example, in query items or on-site pages, with the objective of creating clicks. Every time the client taps on the PPC promotion, the sponsor pays, and the facilitating stage or distributer brings in the cash. A Google lookout for "fall boots," for instance, will raise organic outcomes to beat by supported outcomes — or PPC promotions.

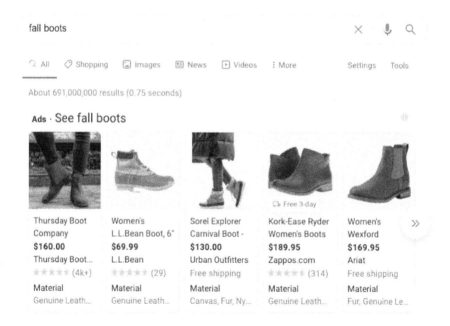

Taboola is also an incredible stage for PPC campaigns, assisting promoters with contacting crowds across premium distributor destinations with suggested articles and recording the drive clients to buy.

2. Social Media

Social stages associate publicists with billions of individuals throughout the world who are prepared to study their number one brands and items. As GlobalWebIndex originate, practically 50% of grown-up Internet clients research items on interpersonal organizations (social networks).

Affiliate advertisers would be astute to utilize social platforms like Twitter, Facebook, and Instagram to share their items, create a following, then click in the trending discussions. Social advertisement capacities permit clients to purchase items directly from the feeds on their walls, so they do not need to leave their applications to drive changes.

3. SEO

SEO (Search engine Optimization) get your site pages ready to be searched by the perfect audiences. By deliberately including mainstream, accessible keywords in your duplicate copy, metadata, and picture labels, you can expand your odds of being found in indexed lists — and drawing in individuals who are searching for precisely what you have to bring to the table.

As per a search from BrightEdge, natural inquiry traffic hopped around 53 percent across ventures in 2019, dominating different channels like online media.

4. Blogging

Writing for a blog is quite possibly the best affiliate marketing advancement technique for different brands. Beginning a blog can help you set up your business's ability, become a go-to hotspot for supportive data, and assemble a local area of perusers who continue to return for more substance.

Take affiliate advertiser GoPro. Their content, "The Inside Line," plunges in the most recent news & "what's going on in the realm of GoPro."

5. Helpful Videos

Online video utilization keeps on soaring as Internet clients are gobbling up social & web live streams and recordings. As Zenith announced, individuals spend a normal of 84 minutes every day watching the web video — and that number is required to arrive at 100 minutes till 2021. That denotes a normal 32% development rate in computerized video utilization from 2013-2018.

Affiliate advertisers can utilize online video to declare new items, direct Q & As, an approach focused crowds, and lead live exhibitions — building intuitive, outwardly captivating encounters for planned purchasers.

For example, affiliate distributer Gear Patrol utilizes its YouTube channel to plunge further into its suggested and viewed items from associate brand accomplices.

6. Coupons

Everybody adores a decent arrangement. Ninety-seven percent of purchasers search for bargains when they shop, and 92% are continually searching for the best arrangement.

Tempt new clients to join the overlay — or reward long-lasting clients for their devotion — by sharing exceptional offers and arrangements that correlate with their inclinations. Famous coupon destinations for affiliate advertisers incorporate Offers.com, RetailMeNot, TechBargains, and Honey.

7. Email Marketing

More than 3.9 billion everyday email clients worldwide, and this number depends on arriving at 4.3 billion by 2023. More than 30% of B2B advertisers even distinguish email bulletins as their best lead-age source.

It's nothing unexpected. Email is a pick in the channel that allows brands & distributors to convey customized content straightforwardly to individuals' inboxes.

Brands can utilize mail showcasing to share altered offers, advance site content, & send clients to their item pages. Online business retailer Bombas, for instance, does this appropriately by sending week-by-week messages custom-fitted to the crowd's interests.

8. Webinars

Much similar to in-person occasions & workshops, online meetings can assist brands with associating their crowds on a more profound level and give a more inside and out gander at what they have to bring to the table. They are additionally an incredible answer for creating email recruits at enrollment and keeping in touch with participants even after the online meeting is finished.

As "GoToWebinar" detailed, email works 57 percent of online meeting enrollments, and 67 percent of enlistments are for an hour-long online meeting, giving a major window to creating client associations.

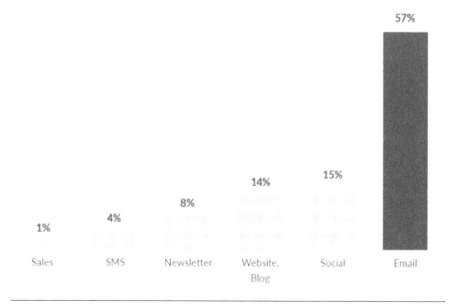

9. Reviews

Audits can represent the moment of truth a brand — and an affiliate marketing effort. Consider that over 91% of individuals read online comments, and 84 percent believe them however much they would like proposals from companions.

That is the reason it's significant for affiliate advertisers to guarantee they deal with their pages' reviews on websites like Yelp and Google by replying to clients and giving impetuses to leaving reviews. Advertisers can likewise band together with affiliate distributors, who can compose reviews on their items and give modified site links to tap and buy.

Take BuzzFeed, which fabricated an entire site around giving reviews to affiliate items.

If you require capitalizing on your publicizing endeavors, you require affiliate advancement strategies to spread the news. You can utilize the systems plot above to begin and construct a multi-channel advancement program, guaranteeing you approach the correct crowds linked to affiliate marketing.

Chapter 14: Money you can earn while working as an affiliate marketer?

The straightforward answer to this is it has no restriction. This relies upon your specialty and the measure of the amount of work you do here.

The best affiliate advertisers make six/seven figures per month.

For instance, Pat Flynn from Passive Smart Income made higher than 100,000$ in commissions of affiliate during Dec 2017.

SPI Income Reports Data 2016–2017 : 2017 12	Link	Current Month
Net Earnings		**$125,819.91**
Gross Earnings		**$166,559.31**
Affiliate Earnings		**$105,619.13**
AWeber	http://www.sm	$1,305.32
Best Year Ever by Michael Hyatt	http://www.sm	$22,259.60
Bluehost	http://www.sm	$27,650.00
ConvertKit	http://www.sm	$36,956.18
Create Awesome Online Courses	http://www.sm	$3,880.00
LeadPages	http://www.sm	$6,294.77
Market Samurai	http://www.sm	$261.12
SamCart	http://www.sm	$1,203.50
Social Media Marketing World	http://www.sm	$300.00
Teachable	http://www.sm	$5,468.44
WP-Wishlist	http://www.sm	$16.20
Bonjoro	http://www.sm	$24.00

Another associate advertiser, Ryan Robinson, revealed more than 19,000$ in affiliate income in October of 2019. Another fruitful affiliate site, "The Wirecutter," created an expected 10 million dollars in income and was ultimately offered to the New York Times for 30 million dollars.

Remember, however, that these individuals have worked hard structuring their brand products. It has taken them long stretches of difficult work to arrive at this point.

You are required to deal with your assumptions. You will not procure gobs of cash first thing, yet don't allow this to debilitate you.

The accomplishment of others discloses to you that with difficult work, the correct information, and time you also can conceivably arrive at those levels.

These simple seven steps should be followed.

1. **Decide on the platform**

2. **Choose the niche**

3. **Find some affiliate programs for joining**

4. **Create great content**

5. **Drive traffic to your affiliate site**

6. **Get clicks on the affiliate links**

7. **To sales, convert the clicks**

14.1 Step No. 1: Decide on the platform

Hypothetically, you can practice affiliate marketing at any stage, even Instagram functions.

In any case, it is a lot simpler to assemble a group of people and increment your associate deals through one of these channels: a YouTube or blog channel.

Beginning a blog now is moderately simple & modest. A lot of instructional exercises online show you how to begin. The most amazing aspect? It'll probably just expense you a couple of dollars each month.

When your website is up, advance it for web crawlers, so you have a superior possibility of positioning. From that point, you're allowed to add associate joins in your substance. (There is an artistry to doing this, which we'll cover later in this guide.)

The alternate platform is YouTube. Making and transferring substances to YouTube is cost-free, which makes it ideal for some individuals. Streamline your recordings for SEO and incorporate associate site links in your depiction.

One of my number one models is at BookTube, where different YouTubers survey books:

Note this you'll have to unveil the way that you're adding associate connections. The FTC (Federal Trade Commissions) expects you to be straightforward while accepting payments from support.

In case you are doing it on YouTube, remember it for your portrayal:

I drink GFUEL (affiliate link):
https://gfuel.ly/31Kargr

My Setup (affiliate links):
Chair: https://clutchchairz.com/pewdiepie/
Official Razer hardware:
Razer Nari Ultimate headset: http://rzr.to/pdp-razer-nari
Razer Customs phone cases: http://rzr.to/pdp-razer-case

NordVPN DOWNLOAD (affiliate link):
Go to https://NordVPN.com/pewdiepie or use code PEWDIEPIE for a special holiday deal. Get a 3-year plan with 81% off plus two amazing gifts: 4 extra months + NordPass password manager app (worth $194.61)

Presently, you'll probably get a bigger number of views from a blog than a YouTube video. Thus, the vast majority of the models going ahead will also be for a blog.

14.2 Step No. 2: Choose the niche

Face this: If you are beginning some blog at present, you are confronting a big rivalry load. Statista measures that the number of bloggers in the U.S will arrive at 31.7 million by the end of 2020.

For having the best potential for success of achievement, specialty down.

Pick a theme that centers around some particular classification. As an example, the subject of "food" is a gigantic class. Instead of handling that, stab at something extra explicit, like barbecuing food.

Keeping the themes tight can help you fabricate a more engaged crowd and possibly assist you in ranking the highest in web indexes.

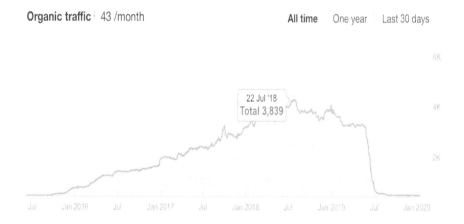

Latterly, as you finished the main part of this class and construct traffic to these pages, you can venture into different zones.

Presently, you'll be the principal content maker. Pick something you are keen on.

A lot of affiliate websites bite the dust because of the absence of consistency. Hence at any rate, in case you're enthusiastic about a subject, you will see it a lot the same to press on when hard times arise.

Try not to stress in case you are not a specialist in the field. As Gary Vaynerchuk said, "record, don't make." Documenting what you have realized can make incredible substance and draw in individuals who are keen on after your success.

If you're re-appropriating the substance, at that point, it's smarter to work with prepared specialists in the field. Specialists might help you make reliable work and quality, which can prompt further traffic, guests, and further associate links.

14.3 Step No. 3: Find affiliate programs to join

There are three kinds of affiliate projects to browse from.

A. Lucrative, affiliate programs of low volume

These are specialty item's associate projects with higher payouts.

E.g., ConvertKit's affiliate project pays nearly $700 each month in the event that you send only 80 clients their way. But, as they are selling CRM programming for entrepreneurs, there is a restricted crowd of clients.

There additionally will be more rivalry for programs with higher commissions. Since you are presumably beginning, it will be much testing to make a significant cash measure going against the gifted advertisers with the profound pockets.

B. High-volume Low-paying affiliate projects

These are projects for things with fewer payouts but mass allure.

E.g., in PS4 games, many play PS4, and the expense of a game is around 50 dollars, and associate commissions are in single digits ordinarily. This implies you will acquire $2 to $3 for each deal in case you are fortunate.

The saving grace of projects like this is that they generally offer great loads of items for selling. Take the partner program of Amazon. You will acquire up to 10% commissions on nearly everything Amazon sells.

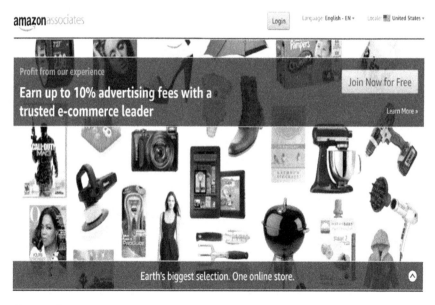

The other beneficial thing is which you frequently get commissions on the whole estimation of the buy instead of simply the item you suggested.

To make these sorts of subsidiary projects pay, you'll need loads of traffic.

C. Lucrative, high-volume affiliate projects

These are some associate projects for items with mass allure, which likewise pay higher commissions.

One model is bank credit cards.

Everybody needs a bank credit card & the vast majority stay with the organization for quite a long time (at times, even many years).

The drawback of these items is that they pull in affiliate advertisers with several aptitude & profound pockets—some similar use malicious techniques that you cannot rival.

Below are the step-by-step instructions for choosing the affiliate projects for signing up.

This relies on your specialty and level of ability.

In case you're focusing on customers, you'll probably go with the 2nd type of lower commissions & higher deal volume.

In case you are pursuing a business crowd, you'll probably go for the primary model: lucrative & low volume. The most famous projects here are for programming and web facilitating related items.

Affiliate Earnings	$19,076.08
Bluehost	*$13,630.00*
OptimizePress	*$156.40*
Kinsta	*$0.00*
Dreamhost	*$500.00*
HubSpot	*$500.00*

An ideal approach to discover these associate programs is with a Google search.

best software affiliate programs

The 67+ Best Affiliate Programs of 2019 (Highest Paying)
https://www.forexreferral.com › best-affiliate-programs ▾
Sep 24, 2019 - Our picks for the **best affiliate programs** to make money online, ... website builders and point of sales **software** providers in the the world.

Best Software Affiliate Programs: Where to Find and How to ...
https://www.amnavigator.com › blog › 2018/09/18 › best-software-affiliat... ▾
Sep 18, 2018 - Again, there are many other **software** brands that chose to keep their **affiliate programs** in-house, and the above list represents only a few of the **top** brands that do so.

Software Affiliate Programs - High Paying Affiliate Programs
https://highpayingaffiliateprograms.com › software-affiliate-programs ▾
Software has the highest margins in the affiliate marketing business. Here are the **best software affiliate programs** available today.

105 Best Affiliate Programs of 2020 (High Paying for Beginners)
https://www.adamenfroy.com › best-high-paying-affiliate-programs ▾
Your ultimate guide to the 105 **best affiliate programs** (ranked and reviewed) to ... Most recurring programs are **software** as a service (SaaS) advertisers whose ...
Affiliate Advantage · Bluehost Affiliate Program · Web Hosting

Then again, enter a contending member site into Ahrefs' Swebite Explorer & go to Linked areas report.

For instance, it must be realized that Pat Flynn advances various programming items on his site, Smart Passive Income. Eyeballing the associated spaces report tells us that Pat connects to Aweber pretty regularly.

overcast.fm ▾	83	6,437	14,714	14	28,356	1,733 ▾
play.google.com ▾	95	18	1,652,821	219,562	438,491,599	1,195 ▾
aweber.com ▾	90	1,271	51,013	2,692	156,28	516 ▾
ziprecruiter.com ▾	85	3,483	15,216	846	6,774,913	495 ▾
lynda.com ▾	86	2,819	37,781	686	811,313	454 ▾
geni.us ▾	83	5,539	16,719	677	4,974	397 ▾
amazon.com ▾	95	23	2,895,249	3,266	715,917,490	398 ▾

Tapping the "Connections from target" caret uncovers that Pat is an associate.

It just takes a snappy Google search for discovering an application structure for this project.

In any case, if there's an item you would truly prefer to advance without a public associate program, contact the organization and inquire as to whether they would fabricate an affiliate association with you.

14.4 Step No. 4: Create great content

In the event that you need your affiliate website to become successful, you are required to make great substance where your affiliate site links fit normally.

Here is a model. Tim Ferriss met more than celebrated individuals and posed them this inquiry:

What acquisition of 100 dollars or less has most certainly affected your life over the most recent half-year (or in ongoing memory)?

Someone distributed the appropriate responses in a blog entry and included partner connects to the items referenced:

Kelly, Kevin: I recently upgraded to a Team/Family plan for 1Password the password management tool. Now all the security, ease, and relief of a good password system can be shared with all my family and people I work closely with. We can safely share appropriate passwords.

Based on the remarks, all his fans adored this.

This is one of the things that you need to imitate when making content for your associate site.

Don't simply aimlessly minister items from Amazon's successes. Go further mile to ensure the substance tackles the concern of the guest.

You can generally begin with what you already have at your home on the off chance that you do not have the cash to buy each item. For instance, if you had a technology blog, you'd make surveys on the devices you have.

14.5 Step No. 5: Driving traffic to your affiliate site

You've made extraordinary substance. This subsequent stage is to get more individuals to understand it, so they'll tap on your partner's site links.

Here you have three different traffic methodologies to consider:

Paid traffic

This is the place where you pay for traffic to your website. You can practice this utilizing PPC promotion.

The benefit of paid traffic is that the second you begin paying, you get traffic.

In any case, there are a few disadvantages.

Running promotions will dive into your benefits. It is typical for the publicists to lose the cash before making it if they at any point do.

You must be sensible regarding what amount of time it requires to streamline a paid traffic crusade.

Also, when you leave paying for promotions, your traffic will stop.

As a rule, promotions are an incredible traffic procedure in case you're important for lucrative affiliate projects and can create the working of numbers.

In any case, you're a novice to paid advertising and have no promoting financial plan at that point, and it probably won't be a particularly good thought.

B. Search engine optimization (SEO)

The act of streamlining pages to rank high in web crawlers like Google.

However long one may rank higher in web crawlers for the objective catchphrases, he/she will get reliable & detached traffic.

On the much essential level, SEO is all about:

Getting knowledge of what your objective clients are looking for.

Making content about those points (item pages, blog entries, and so forth).

Caretaking of the "specialized " stuff to push pages like these high in the web indexes (which include referencing of third-party).

C. Build an email list

The Email records permit you to speak with your perusers whenever.

Utilize them to educate fans concerning new substances and keep them returning to your site for additional. This prompts more associate taps and deals.

You can also send offshoot email advancements to the rundown straightforwardly:

Hey, it's Ryan here...

And yesterday, my friend and mentor Lisa Sasevich opened the doors to her Speak To Sell Training program...

Where she'll be walking you through her EXACT process for creating your own high converting talk for presenting to audiences.

==> **Click here to register**

For assembling the email show, it is needed to convince the perusers on the site to join. It implies offering important something.

At Ahrefs, it is shown in slide box toward the finish of each article:

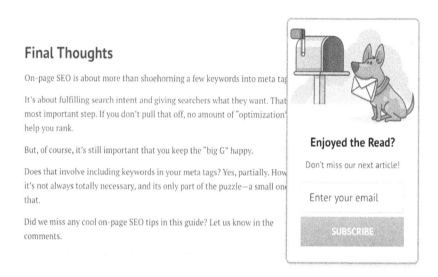

A few sites similar to Gear Patrol additionally have "subscribe" site links on their route bar:

Yet, there are a lot of approaches to do this. You can likewise offer a free eBook, an email course, and so on

All you require is some innovativeness.

14.6 Step No. 6: To sales convert the clicks

Because you've got an astonishing piece of substance does not mean individuals will tap on your associate links.

There are a couple of things you must consider.

A. Link placement

If your associate site links are at the lower part of the page where individuals infrequently scroll, snaps will be rare.

Then again, make each other word a connection in your presentation, and your substance will look nasty.

It would be best if you offset the site link position with different factors beneath.

B. Context

Suppose you were composing context on the famous kitchen blades for below 50 dollars.

Your presentation presumably should not resemble others.

The connections watch inappropriately and malicious.

C. Callouts

Utilizing callouts like fastens, boxes, and tables can assist attraction in your perusers' consideration and make the post more skimmable.

For example, the Wirecutter uses eye-getting boxes with the item interfaces when they share some top pick.

Chef's knife

Our pick

Mac MTH-80

The best chef's knife for most people

With its super-sharp edge, its sleek, tapered shape, and its comfortable handle, this knife will make your everyday dicing and slicing tasks smoother and quicker.

$145 from Amazon

$145 from Cutlery and More

Every kitchen should have a chef's knife—it's the most versatile piece in any cutlery set, and it will make food prep on Thanksgiving and every other day faster and easier. The <u>Mac MTH-80</u> has been the top pick in our guide to <u>chef's knives</u> since 2013, a choice backed by 120 hours of research, interviews with

PC Mag uses a different strategy & utilizations the correlation table with catches:

Product	HostGator Web Hosting	Hostwinds Web Hosting	A2 Web Hosting	DreamHost Web Hosting	AccuWeb Hosting	Liquid Web Hosting	WP Engine Web Hosting	GoDaddy Web Hosting	Cloudways Web Hosting	1&1 Ionos Web Hosting
Lowest Price										
Editors' Rating	●●●●○ EDITORS' CHOICE	●●●●○ EDITORS' CHOICE	●●●●○ EDITORS' CHOICE	●●●●○ EDITORS' CHOICE	●●●●○ EDITORS' CHOICE	●●●●○ EDITORS' CHOICE	●●●●○ EDITORS' CHOICE	●●●●○	●●●●○	●●●●○ EDITORS' CHOICE
Best For	Shared Hosting	Reseller and VPS Hosting	WordPress	Cloud Hosting	Dedicated Hosting	Managed Hosting	WordPress Hosting	Customer Service	Cloud Hosting	Cloud Hosting
Shared Hosting	✓	✓	✓	✓	✓	✓	—	✓	—	✓
VPS Hosting	✓	✓	✓	✓	✓	✓	—	✓	—	✓
Dedicated Hosting	✓	✓	✓	✓	✓	✓	✓	✓	—	✓
WordPress Hosting	✓	✓	✓	✓	✓	✓	✓	✓	—	✓
Cloud Hosting	✓	✓	✓	✓	✓	✓	✓	—	✓	✓
Reseller Hosting	✓	✓	✓	—	✓	✓	—	✓	—	—
Linux Servers	✓	✓	✓	✓	✓	✓	✓	✓	✓	✓
Windows Servers	✓	✓	✓	—	✓	✓	—	✓	—	✓
24/7 Support	✓	✓	✓	✓	✓	✓	✓	✓	✓	✓
Read Review	HostGator Web Hosting Review	Hostwinds Web Hosting Review	A2 Web Hosting Review	DreamHost Web Hosting Review	AccuWeb Hosting Review	Liquid Web Hosting Review	WP Engine Web Hosting Review	GoDaddy Web Hosting Review	Cloudways Web Hosting Review	1&1 Ionos Web Hosting Review

Step #7: Convert clicks to sales

In associate promoting, two transformations need to occur for you to bring in cash.

The principal transformation is the taps to the item page.

You are 100 percent in charge of the activity. Use the strategies above to improvise your chances of getting this click.

The subsequent change is the guest buying the item. On account of member promoting, the dealer controls the checkout & their transformation rates are not in your control.

Always try to play the game for your potential benefit and search for traders with programs that convert well.

Here are a couple of approaches for their discovery:

A. Public income reports

If the individuals are bringing in fair cash from an associate program, at that point, the item changes over well.

How can you say whether individuals are bringing in cash?

Take a gander at public pay reports where bloggers freely uncover how much cash they're making from their member bargains.

You can discover these reports on Google.

For instance, if you look for "money report amazon member," you will see a couple of blog entries indicating how bloggers have brought in cash from Amazon Associates.

Get an in-depth view of your earnings - Amazon Associates
https://affiliate-program.amazon.com › welcome › topic › reports ▾
View detailed **reports** on your **earnings** and boost performance by learning what's working best for you.

How I Made $8,000 IN SEPTEMBER with Amazon's Affiliate ...
https://www.pajamaaffiliates.com › how-made-8000-september-with-amaz... ▾
Lesley here. Notice anything different? No, I'm not lost... I've decided from this time on that I will be posting my **income report** for **Amazon's Affiliate** Program ...

How I made $22,288 from my blog - Income Report May 2019 ...
https://healthysavvyandwise.com › blog-income-report-may-2019 ▾
Jun 23, 2019 - Check out my passive **income report** from my blog in May 2019. I share the key ... You will notice that my #1 **affiliate** is Amazon. Yes, **Amazon**.

Amazon Affiliate Marketing: How to Earn $1,000/Mo (on the ...
https://www.ryrob.com › Blog ▾
Sep 6, 2019 - I'm breaking down exactly how I use **Amazon affiliate** marketing to earn an extra $1000/mo in side **income** for my business. If you're considering ...

It would appear that one blogger made $7,300 in a solitary month from commissions of Amazon.

Income Report – May 2019

Revenue:

Affiliate:

- Amazon $7,312 (no, it's not a typo) see above
- RewardStyle $3,312 (a new record)
- Hometalk $529
- Stupid Simple SEO $356 (yes, I love this name and it's the only other SEO course I recommend)
- Pinteresting Strategies and Affiliate Marketing for bloggers $128

In case you're in a similar space, you can likewise investigate where her other partner pay comes from and possibly advance similar items.

B. Ask questions

In the event that there isn't a lot of data accessible about an associate program, you need to sign up, join and pose inquiries.

For instance, you should discover their normal transformation rates or a rough approximation of their top workers' month-to-month commissions.

This can help you sort out if the subsidiary program merits advancing.

C. Use your intuition

Now and again, it's ideal to go with your hunch.

In the event that the program or item you are looking at feels "off," or whether you'll by and by never prescribe the item to a companion or relative, at that point, don't advance it.

Not any affiliate marketing cycles were re-examined here. These are the basics, and applying these will get you off on the correct foot.

Don't expect extraordinary pay or the opportunity to stop your 9–5 short-term. Affiliate marketing requires some investment.

The spotlight first on generating the first affiliate deal. As your site develops, set new objectives, and keep testing.

This is how to develop a site that ultimately creates fair pay.

Chapter: 15 Tips to become a successful affiliate marketer

If you follow these ten measures, they can help boost the odds of success, whether you are just beginning or are experienced in affiliate marketing. Each tip offers insight into the strategies utilized by the most influential marketers in the industry.

15.1 Your Content Must be Solid

You will need to produce reliable material if you aim to earn extra money from affiliate marketing. There is content in any piece of correspondence you use. You would require the experience of both insightful and relational calls to action and the ability to articulate in a widely readable manner. You will need to make your content easily readable. Answer their queries and provide them with comprehensive knowledge, but present in a available style and interacting. Look at what attracts them to your page. Recognize your audience. A search box is a perfect place to discover on the page what they want to know.

15.2 Track success in your affiliate marketing

Ongoing achievement requires insights into what has happened in history. While you don't want to establish it and forget it- it's crucial to know how guests interact with your website. Search ranking will have an influence, as will online communication, etc. To discover more about your guests, you must use your guest insights. What proportion of visitors is recent versus returning visitors? Which sites get the bulk of your traffic? What links are clicked in your menu bar and other places on each page? Each of these questions can provide responses that you will use to strengthen and add behavior. Where do you get your transfer traffic from? What pages are most visited prior to a transformation? To decide what new content is required or also where to put those links on current websites, use the insights to get answers you will use—using your details.

15.3 Know your products

Information may differentiate you from your rivals. As an associate, you sell different items to your guests, so you need to be known as an authority, or at least a position to provide accurate details on the products you support, to stick out. Affiliates too frequently catch a few sellers without having to meet them, which they believe would be of benefit to their guests. Even if these apps are not tested, you do want to know how they function and what advantages they will provide consumers with. Don't sign up simply because they seem to sell something in your niche - do your analysis on a different vendor.

Look at the feedback that others have given, to begin with, but try to use it yourself, even though it's only a demonstration.

15.4 Engage your visitors

Most popular marketers of affiliates communicate with their guests. Enable feedback if you have a forum. This will give you a chance for your guests to have a discussion. Yeah, you may need to weed out the bots, but they will appear and resume the discussion if you answer to several of your commenters and start discussions.

At the close of a blog article, raise some questions. What other aspects should have been included? "Would you like to learn more about this subject?" "Give your opinion to us!" These campaigns will further encourage engagement with the community. When reacting, use the name of the commentator wherever you can.

15.5 Concentrate one niche affiliate business

So often, affiliate advertisers employ a shotgun tactic to promote as many items as necessary while concentrating on their core concern and matters relating to their niche. Only stick with one niche if you want to grow a profitable affiliate marketing platform. In order to support other niches, you should build other pages, but just don't spread yourself too thin since it can contribute to thin sites with content.

15.6 Provide information and support, instead of sale

Marketing and self-promotion platforms never gain momentum. In order for the visitors to keep coming back, you need to support the clients and have quality data that they consider appropriate. If you look at the websites that score high in your niche with the different words used, you will see that valuable knowledge wins out. Do your analysis to have further knowledge or revised data.

15.7 Always be testing and improving

You should always improve your method: test duration, scheme usage, different sort of art, and other factors. Affiliate marketing is a continuous effort, like every education process. Although all of the above measures can be followed at the outset, you want to understand and develop as you move forward.

15.8 Set proper expectations

In a month, you really aren't going to earn a million dollars. There are reasonable goals you need to create. Some affiliates invest a certain amount of time constructing their initial pages, then commit to a lesser amount when launching a new platform to keep adding material. If you've had a single site of constantly focused construction or a variety of originally smaller sites, set targets and strive to achieve them.

Chapter: 16 Strategies to Increase Your Website Traffic

Following are the strategies to increase your website traffic.

16.1 Amazon affiliate program

The Amazon affiliate program can be a simple way to monetize your blog or website. It is also called "Amazon Associates". Just sign up, gain approval quickly, and today set affiliate links on your blog. You get the commission if somebody makes Amazon purchase from one of your links.

16.2 How Amazon's affiliate program work

Amazon Associates is simply a marketing program that pays website referral incentives. So, you get a portion of the sale of whichever they buy over the next 24 hours anytime you send a consumer to Amazon through a link on your website.

However, the commission depends based on what kind of item a customer buys. In order to see what Amazon's set regular program fee rate is for different product types, refer to the figure below.

Product Category	Fixed Standard Program Fee Rates
Luxury Beauty, Amazon Coins	10.00%
Furniture, Home, Home Improvement, Lawn & Garden, Pets Products, Pantry	8.00%
Headphones, Beauty, Musical Instruments, Business & Industrial Supplies	6.00%
Outdoors, Tools	5.50%
Digital Music, Grocery, Physical Music, Handmade, Digital Videos	5.00%
Physical Books, Health & Personal Care, Sports, Kitchen, Automotive, Baby Products	4.50%
Amazon Fire Tablet Devices, Amazon Kindle Devices, Amazon Fashion Women's, Men's & Kids Private Label, Apparel, Amazon Cloud Cam Devices, Fire TV Edition Smart TVs, Amazon Fire TV Devices, Amazon Echo Devices, Ring Devices, Watches, Jewelry, Luggage, Shoes, and Handbags & Accessories	4.00%
Amazon Fresh, Toys	3.00%
PC, PC Components, DVD & Blu-Ray	2.50%
Televisions, Digital Video Games	2.00%
Physical Video Games & Video Game Consoles	1.00%
Gift Cards; Wireless Service Plans; Alcoholic Beverages; Digital Kindle Products purchased as a subscription; Food prepared and delivered from a restaurant; Amazon Appstore, Prime Now, Amazon Pay Places, or Prime Wardrobe Purchases	0.00%
All Other Categories	4.00%

It's important to remember that not the only factor in your commission is the portion of the sales you get. Your conversion rate also counts because it signifies how many individuals can click an affiliate link and buy the product after viewing your web.

Your conversion rate is the percentage of your website users who make a purchase out of the total number of visitors to your site through your affiliate link. For example, if your website received 5,000 visitors in this month and 10 of those visitors bought the product after clicking on your affiliate link, it will be a 0.2 percent conversion rate.

16.3 How to become an Amazon affiliate

It is an easy process to register with the Amazon Associates program. To begin with, simply visit **https://affiliate-program.amazon.com** and click on "Free Join Now."

First, you may need to input details regarding your account, including your name, phone number and address. You will then be asked to enter banners, advertising or affiliate links on the websites and smartphone app URLs where you want to display them. Up to 50 websites and cumulative smartphone app URLs can be entered.

You can choose a store ID in the following section and provide information, as outlined below, about your websites or smartphone applications and what kind of items you wish to promote.

What are your websites or mobile apps about? *

! This field is required

What can users do on your website or mobile app, who is it for, and what kind of products do you intend to promote?

Which of the following topics best describes your websites or mobile apps? *

| Books | ⁝ |
| Education/ School /Reference/News | ⁝ |

Add Another Topic

What type of Amazon items do you intend to list on your websites or mobile apps? *

☐ Books   ☐ Clothing, Shoes & Jewelry   ☐ Computers & Office
☐ Digital Downloads   ☐ Electronics   ☐ Health & Beauty
☐ Home & Garden   ☐ Kindle   ☐ Movies, Music & Games
☐ Sports & Outdoors   ☐ Tools, Auto & Industrial   ☐ Toys, Kids & Baby

What type are your websites or mobile apps? *

| Select primary type | ⁝ |
| Select secondary type | ⁝ |

Add Another Type

You can also select the topics that better represent your websites or smartphone applications from a dropdown list, such as clothes, books, games or movies.

First, you would need to explain how you push traffic to your websites, how your websites and apps generate income, how you usually develop links, and how many unique visitors you receive on a monthly basis in general.

Traffic & Monetization

How do you drive traffic to your website(s)? *

- [ ] Paid Search
- [✓] Email
- [ ] Shopping Portal
- [ ] Offline

- [ ] Display Advertising
- [ ] Social Networks
- [ ] Forums
- [ ] Rebate

- [ ] SEO
- [ ] Blogs
- [ ] Lead Generation
- [ ] Other

How do you utilize your websites and apps to generate income? *

| Select primary | ⬍ |

| Select secondary | ⬍ | Add Another

How do you usually build links? *

| Select | ⬍ |

How many total unique visitors do your websites and apps get per month? *

| Select | ⬍ |

What is your primary reason for joining the Amazon Associates Program? *

| Select | ⬍ |

How did you hear about us? *

| Select | ⬍ |

You simply have to input your phone number after this section is complete, press "Call Me Now," and respond when you receive a phone call from Amazon. You will be told to enter a four-digit PIN, then set up your account.

You may select whether to input your payment and tax details now or later from here and then continue to your dashboard to start making affiliate links for Amazon.

16.4 Creating affiliate links

The most popular way of creating an associate link is the Product Link Tool. Simply press "Product Linking" at the edge of the Amazon Associates dashboard to reach it and choose "Product Links,"

16.5 SiteStripe tool

The SiteStripe tool helps to create an affiliate link directly from the Amazon product page of any item. If you have set up your Amazon Associates profile, as long as you are logged into the account, the tool would automatically appear at the top of every Amazon.com page.

For using SiteStripe, visit any Amazon product page for the product you would like to create an affiliate link for.

At the top of the list, the SiteStripe bar allows you to create many wide varieties of links. As explained above, you can build a native ad or get a plain-text link, an embedded link image, or a text plus image ad. On Facebook or Twitter, you may also click to upload.

The ad code will appear in a box under there once you have chosen the sort of affiliate link you like, and you will copy the code and paste it on your social network or website.

16.6-Click Bank Products

Clickbank has a collection of more than 4,000 exclusive items that attract more than 200 million worldwide consumers. Clickbank is an e-commerce site that ties more than 6 million digital content producers and affiliate advertisers, who then sell them to buyers. The platform runs via an affiliate network, making it easier for its verified consumers to improve their exposure and promote more customers with their e-books, web classes, images, and songs.

How to use items from ClickBank with your affiliate marketing

- You will also serve as an agent and market items listed by other sellers, along with selling your own items on Clickbank. You will automatically search the numerous items available for you to offer as soon as you sign up to become a Clickbank affiliate. Clickbank has more than 4,000 unique items on the platform; it might be useful to nail down the quest by searching for the type of commodity and/or profit percentage at the start.

- Prior to supporting their offering, it is necessary to closely examine the supplier's sales page. They will give a 75 percent commission rate, but you would not be able to produce revenue regardless of how much traffic you push their website if their website does not seem reliable.

- Un-likely affiliate platforms, Clickbank is a place for all individuals who make content & for the affiliate marketers as well.

Marketing of Clickbank Products/Items

- You must have a webpage that features other partner deals close to the items you choose to advertise from Clickbank, to begin with. WordPress provides a free edition of the content management system (CMS) if you don't have a domain, which you used to start posting blogs instantly.

- Get the readers' attention; you should use your posts and then show your Clickbank affiliate bid anywhere inside the post. You should also create a newspaper and use it as much as possible to advertise your Clickbank deals to your customers.

It is also a choice to create a fan page on Facebook, as most users are also on social networking sites. With the information that connects to your website, you can upload stuff on your Facebook and use it to push traffic to your website. The usage of other content-sharing networks, like Taboola or Outbrain.

Drive Traffic to Your Website

- The more visitors your website achieve, the more cash you will earn with Clickbank. You can invest some time defining phrases that are widely searched for that relate to the item you want to market to optimize your traffic. You can also get some traffic from search engines if you generate articles as well as other material focused on certain keywords, specifically if you hit lengthy search terms.

Instead of one or two sentences, Lengthy keyword terms are longer and much more descriptive search expressions. For starters, if you plan to advertise an online gambling course, you could do some keyword analysis and determine that there is too much rivalry from established websites for the phrase "online poker course." However, there is not as much rivalry in an article focused on addressing the query "When to push during a sit-n-go?" and which might produce more traffic.

Optimize your website

and capture visitor information. The most critical aspect is to guarantee that your site is responsive and does not make any errors, whether you are marketing your own goods or anyone else's material.

You would probably want to start collecting the details of customers who frequently visit your website as quickly as possible. Offering a subscription is one approach to do this. You will create a loyal following with a newsletter to promote all of your deals in the future.Exploring the page

The general Process of Exploration

 Choosing a niche/category that you are acquainted with straight away and browsing items inside it would be suggested by several individuals. Although we agree with this plan for good reasons, we don't think it should be the initial step. Just go ahead and click the option besides the search bar "magnifying glass" without entering something.This will help you to access a comprehensive list of all types of items. You will be using the dropdown menu 'Sort Results by' to arrange the data as per the variety of different parameters. We will hold it set as "Popularity" for our reasons for now, but we still urge you to arrange it by "Gravity" and search through items that way. Forget groups, niches, and everything else at this point. We just want to describe what makes a nice product.

But what do they want to say using this words? High gravity implies that several affiliates make money for that object, or it is a "proven" commodity.

Maybe you think it's a no-brainer, correct? Simply arrange by the highest gravity and select one of those products. Well, it has its challenges, although several suggest taking that path.

The big one is heavy gravity =several affiliates = a bit of rivalry. This isn't necessarily negative, but with people just getting started, this may not be perfect. Navigate through 10-20 high gravity items until we pass on to the next segment. "Visit their product online and page with their "affiliate instruments. Note how they market the goods as an affiliate to both their clients and you In their bid, their funnel, and their sites, you'll begin to find all the most popular ClickBank items that have characteristics in common. You will look for these features of poorly performing goods by studying this. You'll start noticing patterns easily. Usually, the similar characteristics you see amongst these top brands lead greatly to their popularity. We want to learn these features so that in other goods that might be less successful and might be able to get sold, we can identify them. Here are a few items that you could notice: These are a common form of websites that, due to their focus on easily understandable, highly interactive images, transform quite well.

- **Good Tools for Associates**

You can learn that several top brands have devoted sites that let you start marketing their products easily. They also build ready-to-go advertisements for you, video, and models. This illustrates that the retailer worries about recruiting and maintaining associates.

- **Social proof**

- Many goods may provide case studies or other sources of social data that indicate that individuals are successfully utilizing and gaining from that commodity.

- Powerful copying and clear call to action.

You'll certainly notice that if they have a published promotional page, it's really persuasive and keeps drawing you back to learn more. They're often mostly narrative. It would be difficult to skip the purchase now button, and the entire page will call your attention to it, tempting you to purchase it. In the view of the tourist, this leaves a little question on what can be accomplished next.

Choosing the best goods

At this stage, by the examination of top gravity products in all ranges, you must have a basic idea of what a successful product seems like. You must also give any suggestions regarding niches/categories in the ones you want to jump into. While several would point out that fitness, money, and partnerships are always the most lucrative ClickBank niches, you can research depending on what you're involved in and should encourage. It's time to choose a commodity to advertise.

The checklist is here:

Interest in Niche

Passion or huge concentration is a bonus. People truly misjudge this point. You will be drinking, eating & breathing this item niche for many weeks, probably many months and many years to come if it is fruitful, and you jump focusing on rising it. Having an interest in it makes things so much easier and helps you keep going when things get tough.

Gravity does not break the contract

People would advise you to pick a commodity with a gravity rating of at least 30+. It is not, by all means, a law of thumb. As far as the product reaches other aspects of this criterion (and the one in the above section), you should give it a try. Some people have marketed items that had a gravity of 5 and earned decent money.

"Wow" factor and solution to the problem of niches

If your target audience sees this and says instinctively, "I want this!" How did I survive without it? "Then you've achieved a real winner for yourself. In this niche, it helps to be educated so that you can assess this argument quickly.

Great Sales site

Clean, persuasive, and quick to complete checkout.

Affiliate tools

For affiliate assistance, aim to get in contact with the provider. With partner sponsorship, successful retailers will be timely and demonstrate to you that they value you because they earn money when you do.

Chapter 17: Top 10 Affiliate Marketing Niches

Are you trying to raise revenue from one of the most lucrative affiliate marketing niches in 2021? Our guide will help encourage your choice. It is crucial for success to locate a lucrative niche in every affiliate marketing company. This reduces the frustration and hardship and strengthens the payoff for the diligent work. After all, you would need to continually pump out material for it in the long run if you intend to monetize your blog with affiliate marketing, so it makes complete sense to spend your time to determine the niche for your blog. Although in this book we have highlighted the top 11 niche markets for affiliate marketing, you must realize that you will make money from affiliate marketing in every niche. Others could be more lucrative than some, but if you flame out from writing about anything you don't like in the first place, it won't really matter. It is not a simple feat to sustain a steady production of blog posts, and there is no lack of blogs that start off high, with one blog post every once in a while, and then dropping off gradually to once a month, and then once almost every other month.

It's a challenging campaign to create a following and monetize it through affiliate marketing; if the enthusiasm in a niche fades out after many months, it is possible that your affiliate marketing venture may not see much sales at all. Tell yourself this: Can I enjoy blogging one year from now regarding this niche? Without lacking motivation, should I actually compose 100 articles for this niche? If there is a definitive yes to your comment, then good for you! Actually, if it's not, it's not the end of the universe because pure enthusiasm alone doesn't earn money. Although love for your writing niche goes a very long way towards continued encouragement to operate your site, there's no denying that it's simple to master to be enthusiastic about it when you start earning money with affiliate marketing. For a second, think about this: how excited would you be for putting anything to work to generate content day after day without getting any incentives for your job?

17.1 The Health Niche

From Unsplash Picture "As the saying goes," The greatest wealth is health" our health is of the highest concern to us. The health and wellbeing sector has expanded its activities and discovered avenues to meet and connect with its community digitally since the invention of the computer. It is now projected that the global healthcare sector is worth about $10tn, which is more than every nation in the world's GDP except for U.S. and China. The desire and necessity to remain active ensure that individuals can still search into anti-aging tactics, nutrition plans, schemes to work out, and more. The demographic is massive in this niche, and there is plenty to go around with. In the nutrition and fitness niche, the good aspect of writing is that you don't really have to be an expert or licensed healthcare professional. It would generate a stronger image of you as an authority in individuals' minds if you possess certain qualifications or have received appropriate accreditations. Still, if you're serious about studying and seeking solutions, you might succeed in the nutrition and fitness niche even without these qualifications. We recommend you, as always, choose a sub-niche. You may learn about meals and diet plans. In this field, identify popular questions and write comprehensive articles clarifying what works and what doesn't work. With the latest and successful items, stay informed. Write a comprehensive description covering all facets of the company and let the audiences know exactly what to expect from using certain objects.

- **Weight Loss:** Design blogs focusing on fitness and eating healthy. You may cover numerous kinds of principles, including food and diet plans. To inspire and empower your community, you may also post stories of losing weight.

- **Healthy diet:** Healthy eating is typically related to weight reduction, although even non-obese humans can eat healthy food. You should establish a blog for everyone that focuses on providing nutritionally balanced food recipes.

- **Fitness Professionals:** You can suggest presenting yourself as a workout lover if you want to exercise and want to benefit while doing something you enjoy doing. You can provide knowledge on nutrients, strength exercises, behavioral planning and programs, and tailored exercise routines for your customers as a wellness guru.

- **Stress Management:** For most, the 9-5 mania is hectic. Business owners' people who career-oriented will be the main demographic, hoping to gain help and suggestions about tackling depression and tying up their lifestyles.

- **Skincare:** Skincare goes past inflammation, itchy skin, and acne treatments. A blog about skincare will help educate its followers about effective ways to take care of their skin while encouraging skincare items' daily usage.

- **Reproductive Health:** This sort of niche blog is directed at mothers and women who are mothers to be. A niche for maternal health would provide factual knowledge regarding pregnancy, child nutrition, infant growth, and other topics relevant to a mother and her child. Health Line has been one of the leading health blogs in 2021, and in the department of balanced eating and weight reduction is performing very well.

17.2 Love and Relationship Niche

To others, affection is a transient idea, but for the most part, everybody wants love. Whether it is the love of God for its humans or romantic love, people love "affection." In partnerships, love builds up. Some people, especially in today's society, which is usually driven by the Internet, find it challenging to establish or sustain a relationship. This niche is currently so profitable that it is priced in the U.S. alone at an incredible amount of $2.5 billion. People are likely to invest their time and finances on a platform that tells them how to pursue love or flirt. You should build a love and friendship site for your affiliate marketing company if you're quite a romantic charmer. You can compose songs, ideas for your first date, how to please an opposite gender, ideas for dinner wear, first date locations, and more. These subjects produce a large number of web searches on Google. In this niche, DatingAdvice.com is a great platform to explore and benefit from. Any sub-niches in the niche of love and relations you must recognize include: Catch-up: Producing material for individuals who are explicitly trying to hook up and meet without the casual devotion related to relationships. Blind Dates: Blind dating websites explore the advantages of asking on blind dates, secure dating initiatives, and helping set up blind dates. Everyday Love: Help people find love from certain aspects of life. They might be close together or in two different part of the world or only planning to create a relationship consisting of online dating first. Relationship Blog: Share techniques with individuals about strengthening their bonds Age: Develop content related to affection such as the seniors, divorcees, teenagers, work, young adults geared to a particular age group. Religion: Build religion-oriented love and relationship material, especially if your spirituality coincides with religious beliefs.

17.3 Personal Finance and Investment Niche

The niche in private finance and investing is more about making money correct and increasing your total wealth. As there are hundreds of avenues to earn profits, this niche is ever-evolving, but nobody has ever covered all the strategies there are. How is this concerning you? This is where you can succeed if you have any knowledge of finance, personal development, the capital sector, the forex market, and other investment schemes. You can make an excellent affiliate marketing company that allows individuals to save and spend their cash in different networks. To succeed in this niche, you do not have to hold a CPA qualification or be a banker. Financial goods, programs, and resources may be checked. Do some extensive analysis and, with credible references, back up the evidence. In the personal finance and investing niche, other sub-niches that you should know include Stock Market: Develop posts that examine the stock market's devices and patterns. Foreign Exchange Markets: Establish articles that compare foreign and major currency pairs. You may also build content that analyses the best dealers and programs for applications. Credit Card Niche and Loan Management: Widely discussed themes are credit card loans and credit card incentives. You should go the extra mile to teach loan handling to your audiences. In the personal finance and savings niche, NerdWallet is an expert. Grab a cue from them and understand how to get going.

17.4 The Pet Care Niche

Do you adore pets? Do you got one? Have you served in the veterinarian department? Pet owners adore their pets and are ready to pay a fortune and provide them with quality pet treatment. Some common pets are Puppies, cats, and possums. A few pet affiliate programs are seeking to collaborate with passionate pet owners, which provides a chance to transform your passion for pets into a profitable affiliate business. Here, find out the top 10 pet niche partner services. Is the niche in Pet Treatment profitable? It is reported that the pet care sector produces over 21 billion dollars worldwide, so it's extremely profitable. Such sub-niches in the pet care niche that you should know include Pet Clothing and Shoes: Assist people who own pets, choose how to dress their pet, and help them decide on the accessories for their pet. You should compose informative articles about trends and services in pet fashion. Pet Grooming: Build material for animal lovers who want to hear more about the best pet hygiene treatment. Animal Diet and Tips: Write material based on nutrition, diets for the beloved pets of your audience, and handmade dishes. In the pet care niche, Herepup is a platform making a fortune.

17.5 The Travel Niche

Every so often, it's an idea that clicks our mind- leave your work, grab a few items, and drive off to a place you've never been. Stuff such as digital invasion, traffic issues, job tension, relationship issues, unemployment, inflation, conflicts, and other anomalies of existence creates a big argument on why there is a need for us to travel. So, an important question arises. How do these nerve-racking conditions bypass us? The perfect answer that turns up in my mind is 'travel.' The travel niche is the best fit for everyone if you are enthusiastic about exploring & intrigued about fresh experiences. For several people, traveling is relaxing, and you can provide them with information about tourist destinations and suggestions. But how do you launch a journal about traveling? People who enjoy traveling the universe and blogging about it maintain the strongest travel blog. You should relive others' travel experiences vicariously if you do not have enough resources to travel just yet. Your analysis capabilities and narrative ability need to be honed. You also need to showcase the most elusive tourist attractions' secret masterpieces. You should even engage guest reviewers so that they can share their travel stories with the audiences. There are different affiliate programs affiliated with airlines, brokers, and tour companies that are able to offer an enticing amount for each person that, via your connection, trades with them. There are multiple partner programs for the travel niche, including Booking.com, Agoda, TripAdvisor, Skyscanner, and Airbnb. Several other independent advertisers will ask you for a marketing drive or an advertising spot. Any sub-niches in the travel niche that you can know include Travel budgeting: When people are traveling, not everybody likes to overspend money. There are a variety of travel tips and ideas that allow people who are traveling on the road to save money. You should write educational blog articles about how travel agencies and corporations can save money and avoid getting scammed. You should also show customers how to use deals and credit incentives with discounts. Backpackers Guide: On a tight budget, backpackers wander around the globe. They enjoy camping, biking, driving, and participating in sports of high octane. Develop articles that help travellers prepare and navigate safer for backpackers. Airplane and Travel Tour Business Reviews: Not everybody loves to indulge in the boring task of preparing themselves for flying. The majority of individuals will like to go by an intermediary or a travel agency. This is where they require your assistance. You may run a questionnaire or obtain details from web pages and compose detailed reviews of these airlines and travel agencies. Livingthedreamrtw is a perfect example of a website for a travel affiliate done correctly. They also have a blog article that you can read here that explains how they were able to make $30,000 a year on sales from affiliates!

17.6. Gardening

Well, it might sound bizarre, but one of the successful niches of affiliate marketing is gardening as well. From the younger times when gardening was seen as a hobby to be undertaken over the weekend or spare time, it has achieved an entirely new stage now. There are many micro-niches within this, which are lucrative with agricultural development. As mentioned earlier, everything is easily accessible on the Internet, and people use Internet-based information and resources to do whatever they want.

The Niche in Fashion and Beauty from Unsplash Picture Fashion depicts what we are wearing and how we are wearing it. When you are looking forward to starting your affiliate marketing company, the fashion niche is extremely profitable. In the luxury sector, brands like Ralph Lauren and Gucci have set the standard. Everyone likes to look stylish, from clothing to boots, shoes, sunglasses, gowns, ties, and other accessories. Whether you want to keep things easy or want to dazzle in a grand design, Fashion is something all of us are passionate about. Beauty objects come under the category of Fashion as well. People enjoy spending money on their skin in order to maintain it flawless and flexible. Now is the perfect moment to be living if you enjoy your Fentys, Yeezys, and b=Balmain. Your fashion niche enthusiasm can be brought to the upper stage. Build a fashion magazine and write exciting posts on developments in Fashion, new launches, the four big weeks of Fashion, and more. Don't keep regurgitating what's out there; express your exclusive vision of stories connected to design. You should know any sub-niches in the niche of Fashion and beauty: Beauty and Cosmetics: Compose factual articles focused on skin type and multiple things to use. Fashion Trends: With every season, there is a trend option. Winter is coming, and the article should be about winter-themed boots, jackets, and blazers. An example of a fashion and beauty site devoted to having others gain inspiration for their apparel and private aesthetics is The Atlantic Pacific.

17.7 Gaming

The gaming market has evolved magnificently with the introduction of gaming computers, tablets, and other smart devices. Sports, regardless of gender or socioeconomic status, are played by citizens of all age-groups. The gaming niche has the benefit that users are constantly refreshing with new updates and continue to be informed of the new material that has arisen. Typically, people get hooked to such games and continue to keep up to date on them. And more and more games are being designed with more innovation and make people go mad. As well as, in today's period, the vast sector has no age or gender bars and enables itself to be a profitable niche.

17.8. Niche for Self-Improvement

From Unsplash Picture Changes in self-improvement can be seen across various regions. Self-improvement is the tendency to be the better version of yourself in your work, relationship, as a parent, companion, or an individual. In self-improvement, there are many essential aspects to cover, and as such, you will have to choose a special niche. You will become a coach to many if you're an expert in a particular area, such as software engineering, copywriting or accounting. As a writer in the niche of self-improvement, the mission is to make content available that is targeted towards people who want to further improve themselves individually in their targeted area. Any sub-niches in the self-improvement niche you may include: Leadership and Public Speaking: Communication skills and management are important aspects of every profession; however, many people are struggling with them. For best impact, write about how to build an acceptable tone and body expression. Presentation

Skills: You will share secrets in presentation preparation that can help your audiences develop connections and impact them right from the beginning. Lifehack.org does a great job at helping individuals develop their communication and intellectual capacities. Lifehack posts the mundane and complicated hacks that can make you become stronger.

Chapter: 18 Top affiliate programs to promote

You have one issue on your list as the affiliate marketer: results. It is worth testing out limited channels to check what fits you to achieve the best results for your affiliate projects. Here are a few fantastic affiliate marketing services for you to try out, whether you're a novice just beginning or more experienced with some knowledge behind you. See what sort of deals can help you make the highest converts on the most common channels and build a stable long-term earning.

18.1 eBay partner network

Here's a decent way to step into the eBay market's big affiliate capacity. On social networking, your website or blog promotes eBay items and gets revenue from any item sold via your connection. It is quick to sign up for the eBay Affiliate Network, and there is an infinite supply of innovative items to promote, including famous fashion items and regular offers.

18.2 Shopify

Shopify is the most successful website maker in the world for e-commerce, with 400,000 retailers and a significant 200 percent discount on paying stores. Stable rates of transformation come with their brand identification. Plus, their platform contains useful FAQs and promotion tips for affiliates.

18.3 Colmex Pro Affiliate program; Summary

What's Pro Colmex? It is an EU-controlled trading business providing immediate execution across six separate channels, up to 1:20 margins on stocks and 1:200 margins on forex. Colmex pro customers tap into managed professionals to leverage their time as acquisitions and business games are made. The Colmex Pro website and services enable investors to discover US markets, FX & resources, and nationwide exchanges and benefit from them. A restriction-free area is granted by the platform to exchange whenever the consumers like.

18.4 ForexClub

This has been around since 1997, with 100 offices dotted around the world. So, they're not exactly a fly-by-night operation. Besides online trading channels, they sell exercise courses also to help both experienced and new Forex traders take their skills and knowledge to the advanced level.

18.5 About Eharmony

Eharmony has more than 20 years of success getting partners together and is among the world's largest serious partnership sites. Eharmony's reputation is second to none, with over half a million partnerships formed in the UK and more than 120,000 weddings over the last decade.

18.6 Objective

This company has been around for more than a decade now, opening the first shop back in 1902. In 1999, Goal.com went live, and soon afterward, the Target affiliate network preceded. Target Homepage Screenshot essentially, and you will not have to justify who Target is to your viewers and why they should suggest interacting with them. As you wouldn't need to pre-sell just as much, there's always a big bonus for associates.

18.7 VigLink

It operates differently than other services for blog monetization. VigLink turns the regular outgoing links into partner links, and you receive a commission letter from it if clients buy a product. The best thing is that you do not have to be registered for a personal affiliate account for all systems.

18.8 Swoop

Swoop is a specially made affiliate company for food websites, and they are awesome! All you have to do is put a code in your page header, and when it detects a specific fit, Swoop can inject an ad inside the material of your web, usually in an article or a recipe. In comparison to your links, you can also opt just to show Swoop advertisements on your recipe cards. Any food blogger should use the Swoop as it is non-invasive, and you're sure to make several dollars every month.

18.9 Sovrn

Sovrn is a CPM-based advertising company that pays based on CPM (cost per thousand). Apparently, you get charged a certain sum of money for every thousand impressions that an ad is shown. To earn cash, viewers to your site do not have to press a button, which is perfect for food bloggers! Since most people browsing food blogs are searching for tips, not items to purchase, I'm suggesting this. So, there's a really poor risk of them tapping on one of your posters. You would be earning peanuts if you're on an advertising network that costs depending on CPC (cost per click), but they'll only compensate when someone opens an ad.

18.10 The Creative business

The Affiliate Plan provides opportunities for 30 days to receive a discount on every single order by all Innovative Market-referred consumers. Affiliate marketing fees may differ, and so can the time period during which a transaction has to be finished. Requests run for 30 days in the Innovative Business Affiliate Scheme, meaning that participants can gain money

from both fresh and repeat consumer orders. A clear 10 percent of the sales price is the fee received from one of those transactions.

18.11 Jane Associate Program

For clothing, jewellery, and other accessories, the Jane clothing company and website offer boutique sales. Jane contains the newest in design styles for females, home decoration, and clothes for kids. To save even further on the highly reduced price of its high-quality goods, the website features daily discounts and promotions. The word Jane has become associated with value, contributing to a loyal client base. The Jane partner scheme offers current revenue commissions at an average of 11 percent and returning consumers commissions of 10 percent. High-quality ad banners, 1,000+ items every day (with 100 new offers per night), deep connecting, and efficient affiliate management are the service's advantages.

18.12 FitBark

The marketing strategy for pet affiliates allows the user to take a commission via your corporation or blog selling FitBark product lines. Journalists, doggie day-cares, dog walkers, coaches, veterinary doctors, and more are perfect associates. FitBark is on a quest to work together to keep dogs and people safe. The FitBark Affiliate Marketing Platform is a platform that provides contributing websites to receive revenue using specially monitored connections on fitbark.com-referred purchases. FitBark partners with ShareASale to tackle the method of affiliate marketing simply and affordably for affiliates. The business offers custom ties and banners for members that they can display on their sites. Then the affiliate gets a fee on the transaction anytime a visitor recommended by an associate makes a transaction on fitbark.com.

18.13 Travelpayouts

Travelpayouts label them "The perfect travel platform to commercialize your website for travel," and you have to agree with that. They cover a variety of facilities and incorporate Booking.com, Airbnb, rentalcars.com, and more. Up to an 80% fee is provided through their travel partner marketing site, although the average is 1.6% for flights and 6% for hotel stays. The length of their cookies is 30 days.

18.14 Rakuten LinkShare Rakuten Affiliate Network

Rakuten, previously known as LinkShare, is a franchises system that has been in business since 1996. They're not as big as CJ by Conversant, but they've been in operation longer than others. They employ approximately 1,000 merchants to select from, though, including several well-known labels such as New Balance, Pac Sun, Ray-Ban, and Sephora.

Conclusion

Affiliate marketing is a decent way to make a living, but there are a number of items to be done before you can start counting your profit earnings. You need to select the good or service you want to advertise, define your target audience's desires, and modify the website for the purposes of affiliate marketing.

Steady passive revenue only follows operations that are well-planned and implemented. Making major efforts across all platforms would help you develop yourself as a trustworthy promoter and reviewer, a role that any affiliate marketer needs.

CPSIA information can be obtained
at www.ICGtesting.com
Printed in the USA
BVHW041013150321
602551BV00006B/478